HOW TO FOLLOW YOUR INSTINCTS ON THE STOCK MARKET

"It's Simpler Than You Think"

By Stephen Roberts and
Annie Roberts

For Dad

I dedicate this book to my father, Clive Roberts, who passed away on March 18, 2018. His hard work and ability to turn his hand to any task, inspired me to write this book. He taught me that anything is possible when we are forced to be innovative.

CONTENTS

Title Page	1
Dedication	3
Prologue	7
Chapter One: Premonition	8
Chapter Two: Instinct	14
Chapter Three: My First Laundromat	18
Chapter Four: It Doesn't Take a Wizard	23
Chapter Five: Tear Up the Spreadsheet	27
Chapter Six: The Times Square Principle	33
Chapter Seven: The Stock Market is Child's Play	38
Chapter Eight: Electrifying Cars	41
Chapter Nine: Autonomous Cars	47
Chapter Ten: The Space Race	51
Chapter Eleven: The Touchless Principle	59
Chapter Twelve: The COVID-19 Principle	69
Chapter Thirteen: The Internet of Things	80
Chapter Fourteen: Your Health is Your Wealth	91
Chapter Fifteen: The Image Principle	101
Chapter Sixteen: Victims of COVID-19	113
Chapter Seventeen: The Ticker Shock	118
Chapter Eighteen: The Greta Principle	121

Chapter Nineteen: The Petroleum Laundromat   131
Chapter Twenty: Don't Get Too Excited About Renewables!   139
Chapter Twenty-One: The Magic Carpet Principle   144
Chapter Twenty-Two: It's OK to Admit You're Wrong   151
Chapter Twenty-Three: The Tipping Point   155
Chapter Twenty-Four: Staying Ahead of the Curve   160
Chapter Twenty-Five: Catching the Next Wave   167
About The Author   173
About The Author   175

PROLOGUE

The stock market isn't daunting. Although many people think it is, trust me, it's not. It's simpler than you think. Throughout this book, I am going to encourage you to view the stock market in a different light. I'm not the typical hedge fund manager you would imagine -- in a suit and tie, behind a desk in an office tower. I sit at home in Jersey, in swimming shorts and flip flops, just observing the world around me. Investment opportunities are everywhere.

All you need to do is think outside the box, observe and -- most of all -- listen to teenagers. I believe in this approach so passionately that I wrote this book alongside my 19-year-old daughter, Annie. We worked with Michael Shari, a journalist in New York, to combine my time-tested investment principles with Annie's teenage instincts into one voice to carry our generational message: Everyone in Annie's generation is the future of investing -- and needs to be listened to.

CHAPTER ONE: PREMONITION

We had no idea what we were getting ourselves into when we planned our four-day skiing vacation in the Dolomites range of the Italian Alps in late February 2020 on Booking.com to celebrate my wife Georgie's birthday – and my early retirement as a hedge fund manager. When we landed in Milan on February 19, our four children were laughing at the three men who appeared to be wearing beekeepers' suits at the far end of a corridor on the way to the immigration counter. When they approached us and aimed red laser beams from their thermometers at our foreheads, we could see that they were actually wearing white hazmat suits that completely covered their faces and the rest of their bodies. It was as if they had landed from outer space. The children couldn't stop giggling. Georgie and I stifled the urge to laugh out loud.

The men in beekeepers' suits, as my youngest son, Henry, called them, were not amused. I asked how long they had been wearing the suits. "Ten days," one of them replied in an Italian accent. I turned to Georgie and said, "Something's wrong here."

They let us pass through immigration. We loaded our skis into a black Mercedes van and laughed at jokes the children cracked about the beekeeping spacemen as our driver threaded his way through the streets of Italy's financial center and then up into the Dolomite Mountains. By the roadside, we saw typically well-dressed Italians going about their daily business.

After we checked into the immaculate Lefay Resort in Pinzolo, with its tall glass windows affording breath-taking views of snow-smothered peaks, we soon found that we were the only party of six at the hotel. We had breakfast in our ski outfits, surrounded by couples on a romantic weekend. They sat in their glamourous red bathrobes occasionally glancing over at our noisy table. We felt slightly out of place. It was strange not to see any other families in the hotel during the winter break from school.

We hired a local guide to show us around. The charming Matteo, with long curly brown hair, was the 22-year old son of a hotel proprietor in Pinzolo, and he knew everyone in town. We never had to stand in line for more than a couple of minutes for a ski lift. He said, "English people like to wait in queues, but we Italians don't."

Matteo would walk straight up to the Italian guy who was helping the smaller children hoist their skis into the gondola, shoot the breeze about their friends and relatives in Pinzolo, and wave us aboard the gondola. None of the other skiers protested. No one knew that Matteo was not a ski instructor and was thus breaking the rules of the resort, which provided an express lane at each lift station for ski instructors and their students to skip the line. It was the closest to insider trading that I was ever going to allow myself to get, so I savored the moment just as I did the bold Amarone red wine we ordered with dinner every evening.

We were always happy to abandon the back of the line, where everyone was standing just inches away from each other. In the tiny, glassed-in gondola, we were packed in tightly, all within a centimeter of each other, feeling like we were on the subway during rush hour. When we mentioned COVID-19, which we had just only heard about before leaving our home on the island of Jersey, Matteo just laughed it off. The virus would never reach us in Pinzolo, where the town was walled in like a fortress by the slopes of the high Dolomites at a safe altitude of 2,600 feet. No, he laughed, we were all perfectly safe up here.

Because our children are all teenagers, they can ski independently, which makes the whole skiing experience much more exhilarating for me and Georgie. Skiing is therapeutic. It clears the mind. You have to concentrate solely on skiing. If you think about the same thing every day – whether it's investing in the stock market or running a laundromat – sometimes you can't see the forest for the trees. At the end of day you are always exhausted. It helps you look at things differently. It changes your perspective on everything.

At dinner, we enjoyed the fine Italian cuisine that the romantic couples had been enjoying as part of their daily routine. While we didn't indulge in Vitello Tonnato, we relaxed over tray after tray of rustic Italian pizza with a thin, square crust, covered with tomato and buffalo mozzarella.

In our hotel room, we watched television news reports about the spread of the novel Coronavirus in China. When people in hazmat suits walked across the screen, this time we all knew they were definitely not beekeepers. China had built the 1,000-bed Huoshenshan Hospital in just ten days for COVID-19 patients. On our fourth day of skiing, the news reported 16 confirmed cases of COVID-19 in Lombardy, which was the region where we were. The first death was on February 22, the day we packed our skis and called a taxi to the airport.

The same driver picked us up in the same black Mercedes van. On the drive back to Milan, many of local deli windows had very little on display. There seemed to be more people queuing outside the shops than we had seen on the drive up to Pinzolo. The people were behaving differently this time. When we stopped to buy water, the locals still seemed unconcerned, and there was little evidence of panic.

"So, what about this virus?" I asked the driver.

"I don't worry about it," he replied. "I'm not from this region."

When we walked into the airport, we heard people at the check-in desk discussing a neighbor who had fallen ill, and another was talking about his uncle being in a hospital 50 miles away.

Then it hit me. I began to recognize a sense of trepidation I had been feeling in my gut from the moment we had landed in Milan when the children had giggled at the three men in hazmat suits. My urge to giggle along with them had been born out of nervous laughter. I had not felt this way since the months leading to the global financial crisis of 2008.

This was a replay of the latter nine months of 2007, prior to which no one had heard the word "subprime" until the U.S. corporate bond market was dragged down in April that year by bonds that were backed by subprime mortgages that had gone into default. Even regulators didn't know what subprime was. However, as the portfolio manager of a hedge fund in London, I saw it as an opportunity to short bank stocks and make a killing for my investors while the S&P 500 fell by 37 percent in 2008.

In February of 2020, all it took was a four-day skiing trip in the Dolomites for me to figure out that the authorities were just as far behind the curve on COVID-19 as they had been on subprime mortgage-backed bonds in 2007. My four children were far more adept at handling the curves in the Dolomites than global leaders were at getting ahead of a global pandemic. A week later, U.S. President Donald Trump returned to Washington from a state visit to India; it would take him another week to start taking "the Chinese virus" seriously. In London, it would take British Prime Minister Boris Johnson a week to start washing his hands on national television long enough to sing happy birthday twice. Boris Johnson naively thought hand washing alone would prevent the deadly virus from spreading.

Before we boarded the plane, we were scanned by the same three men in hazmat suits who had scanned us upon landing. This time, it wasn't funny. As soon as the plane took off, I turned to Georgie and said, "It's a good thing we left when we did. This airport is probably going to shut down."

Georgie, who happens to be a commercial airline pilot, couldn't hold back a sigh of relief as we soared up through the clouds.

By the time the airport actually closed "temporarily" on March 16, and the authorities in Italy understood what they were dealing with, it was too late. It was beginning to look like a global seismic catastrophe. Tremors in Wuhan would lead to a seismic earthquake in Europe, spread to the San Andreas Fault, and eventually the whole world would ice over.

BY STEPHEN AND ANNIE ROBERTS

 Just as I did in 2008, I was determined to get ahead of the curve this time. I knew I had to stay ahead of not only every human analyst and broker on the stock market but also the countless computer banks that manage most of the funds under management in the world today. These computers run inhumanly clever algorithms that can detect a butterfly flapping its wings in Japan, so I knew the next crisis would have to be a curve ball that no algorithm could have measured or modeled for. If the economic consequences of COVID-19 were too complicated for the best software that Wall Street could buy, then automated trading systems from New York to London to Tokyo would instantaneously sell all "risk assets," starting with stocks that anyone had ever hinted were too expensive for any reason whatsoever.

 As in past stock market crashes, the likely suspects would be stocks no less admired than Amazon, which has never fit conveniently into a spreadsheet because its profits never find their way into the pockets of shareholders, and Tesla, which perpetually finds itself in the cross-hairs of skeptics of its cutting-edge automotive technology. The algorithms were no better equipped than Booking.com to alter this course of events. Wall Street was about to hit the de-risk button -- and the result was going to be ugly.

 As soon as I could get behind my desk in Jersey, I hit the button. First, I liquidated the Horseman European Select long-short equity hedge fund, which I had managed for fifteen years. This move was a few days ahead of schedule, as I had planned to wait until the last day of the month to liquidate the fund, formally retire from Horseman at the middle age of forty-seven and start my own family office. Had I waited until the planned date of February 28, my fund would have taken a shellacking as the market started to implode.

 The Euro Stoxx 50 index lost 34.6 percent between February 19, when it plunged into freefall faster than we could ski down the slopes of the Dolomites, and March 18, when it hit rock bottom. When I hit the sell button on the first available trading day,

February 24, the Stoxx 50 had only lost 5.6 percent.

When I launched my family office as planned on March 1, I first shorted the S&P 500, which eventually fell, by 33.9 percent, before bottoming out on March 23. If you had told me three months earlier that, due to a deadly virus, my first trade in my new family office would be a short position in a major index, I would have gawked at you in disbelief. Yet the dramatic sell-off in the markets created a wonderful opportunity to re-invest in some of the best businesses in the world at attractive valuations. I started with Amazon, the American online retailer, which had fallen 22 percent despite an increase in the number of deliveries to those who were afraid to venture outside and risk becoming infected.

I was determined to stay ahead of the curve -- and hopefully come out of the pandemic in an even stronger position than where I had started.

CHAPTER TWO: INSTINCT

I honestly don't know if anyone can be born with the instincts of an investor. I've watched my two Labrador Retrievers, Scottie and Bernie, grow up from puppyhood instinctively chasing every stick I've thrown at them. For as long as I can remember, there was never a single moment when I didn't feel an instinct to plunge every penny I had saved into the stock market. Investing has always felt as natural to me as fetching a stick has felt to Scottie and Bernie.

I've been striving for success since at least the age of twelve, when I started delivering newspapers. I rose to that challenge the same way every morning. John Lennon's house was at the bottom of the road I used to cycle up at the end of my paper route. This last hill was extremely challenging on my BMX, which had no gears. I had to dig my feet deep into the pedals to climb that hill without stopping, starting at John Lennon's house and flying past Strawberry Fields, which the backyard of my house opened onto. Reaching the top of the hill would motivate me for the rest of the day.

I lived on a side street off Quarry Street, which the Beatles originally named themselves after. They started out as the Quarry Men before changing the band's name. I often pondered the unbelievable success of a boy from my neighborhood who had started out with no more than I had.

The Beatles motivated me to succeed. I may never have performed at Shea stadium with thousands of women screaming so loudly that I couldn't hear myself play guitar, but I certainly can lay claim to achieving even more than I ever could have dreamt of. By the time I was 40, to my amazement, I was ranked among the world's top 100 hedge fund managers based on performance alone by Barron's, the financial magazine published in New York. This is something I'm enormously proud of.

No one ever expected me to get that far, of course. Being dyslexic, I was not exactly a highflyer at school. Special Ed didn't exist in Liverpool's schools in the 1980s. If you had a learning disability, the teachers just left you to one side. They thought you were stupid.

Whenever there was a reading lesson, students took turns reading aloud in front of the class of 30 children. I would punch myself in the nose to cause a nosebleed, and the teacher would send me out of the classroom. Even to this day, I feel anxious when someone asks me to read a piece of text out loud.

I was just 12 years old that morning when I tore out an application from one of my customers' newspapers to buy equity in companies that the UK government was privatizing, including British Gas and British Telecom. I could see that the stocks were cheap. I read articles saying that they were being deliberately sold at a discount because Margaret Thatcher's government wanted to get people more involved in the economy.

Too young to buy the stocks under my own name, I bought them in my mother's and father's names with money I had saved from the paper route. The subscriber from whose newspaper I tore out the application must have missed his chance. Then again, he might not have had my foresight or dreams.

Looking back on it, I can see that I was a prodigy of Margaret Thatcher. During the years that Ronald Reagan was pulling the U.S. out of a jobless recession Margaret Thatcher, a Conservative prime minister and the daughter of a grocer from Lincolnshire, ruled over the UK's transformation from a centrally controlled economy to a more market-driven one. Thatcher wanted to invent people like me. In a way, I suppose she succeeded.

My best friend, Jon Hughes, was the son of a toy wholesaler in Liverpool. His father got ahold of a Jumping Castle, what we call a Bouncy Castle in the UK. We figured out that we could raise the money to buy it from him if we rented it out just 10 times. We wrote a flyer offering our colorful "Bouncy Castle" for rent for birthday parties and similar occasions, photocopied it, and inserted it in the newspapers I delivered. Jon's father stored the jumping castle in his garage. My newspaper customers jumped at the chance to rent it. By the end of the summer of 1989, we owned the jumping castle. By the time I left school at the age of 18, I had £3,000 in the bank — equivalent to about $4,750 at the time.

I knew instinctively not to go into the laundromat business with my father, even though I worked for him on weekends. Even at the age of 14, I could feel in my gut that the business had no future. My grandfather and father had bought the Kwikwash chain of seven laundromats in Liverpool in the Seventies. The business was initially very successful. With the demolition of high-rise Council Housing in the middle of town -- what you'd call the Projects in New York -- in the mid-1970s, hundreds of thousands of people who had used those laundromats regularly were relocated outside the city to houses in what became the Liverpool Green Belt. Their new houses were all equipped with built-in washing machines. Despite my dyslexia, I could see there was no way forward.

Still, my father remained wedded to the business. A reserved, very kind man, he was incredibly innovative, always able to complete any practical task. As his laundromat business slowly dwindled even he could not swim against the tide. He also felt such a huge social responsibility for his employees that he just couldn't bring himself to declare them "redundant," as they say at the unemployment office. For my father, running laundromats was like running a charity. He always put his employees before his own welfare.

Perpetuating a business that he knew was failing – with no acknowledgment of its inevitable death -- hardened his face and drew lines in it. It made him walk slower. It wouldn't even let him stand up straight. We never really had a conversation about his dwindling business until he found out that he was dying from cancer of the esophagus, which killed him in 2018.

Even after he passed away, I never viewed my father as a failure. In fact, his laundromats were the last ones standing in Liverpool. He was just stuck running a business that was disrupted by a change in the way people live. He was just trying to support his family the best way he knew.

While I was studying for the A-Level exams – the standardized tests that British students take to qualify for a university -- in biology, physics and chemistry, the career counselor at my school, St. Edward's College Liverpool, advised me, "Do something with your hands."

He got it wrong. I can hardly hammer a nail straight. Today, my children laugh at how badly advised I had been to take three science exams when I had no intention of pursuing a career in any of those fields. It came as no surprise that my grades were not high enough to allow me to study business at City University of London, the only university I was interested in attending because it was in the heart of the financial district.

As a result, at the age of 18, I found myself claiming unemployment benefits from the government while looking for a job. The youth unemployment rate was 30 percent at the time, and I accumulated a stack of rejection letters – even one from a Tesco supermarket, where I had applied for a job stacking the shelves.

Like anyone else on the dole, as we say in England, I was required to meet Job Club counselors every week to prove that I was looking for work. In one meeting, a couple of career counselors asked me and Dave Ramsey, my best friend in high school, what we wanted to do with our lives. I said I wanted to be stockbroker, and Dave said he wanted to be a government bond trader.

They looked at us in disbelief. Everyone else was willing to take any job as long as they could get some money out of it. But here we were, just a couple of dreamers with aspirations. Dave Ramsey, still a friend, now trades government bonds for a top hedge fund. In the words of John Lennon, "You may say I'm a dreamer, but I'm not the only one."

CHAPTER THREE: MY FIRST LAUNDROMAT

In 1991, when I was just 19, I applied for a job at Winterflood Securities, the best-known small-cap market maker in the City of London, founded by the flamboyant and respected Brian Winterflood. I took Georgie, who was then my girlfriend, along with me to the interview. The elevator opened right into the dealing room. The air was thick with the testosterone of 40 blokes at their desks across the floor, all great characters from a diverse cross-section of society.

The heads of dealing at the time, Julian Palfreyman and David Macnamara, interviewed me. We talked about the stocks I had been trading, my paper route, and my jumping castle business, followed by a short discussion about Liverpool Football Club. They asked me why I had brought my 16-year-old girlfriend with me to a job interview.

"We came down from Liverpool on the train, and this is a day out for us," I said.

They thought that was hysterical. They called the next day, said they liked the interview, and hired me as a blue button. This involved running errands all day, buying the dealers new shoes, and even going shopping for their wives' birthday presents.

Winterfloods was unique as they liked hiring people straight out of school and molding them from scratch. They didn't want their employees to have preconceived ideas. They employed people who were keen to fit into the team, were self-motivated, and had a bit of a character. This format proved very successful. Winterfloods is one of the only market-making firms still standing today.

Everyone on the dealing floor had a less-than-flattering nickname, so they had to call me something. There was already a Scouser in the company – Scousers are what people from Liverpool are called – so that had become his nickname. For me, they combined Scouser with Stephen to arrive at Stegsy, which my children sometimes call me even today.

That wasn't even the tip of the iceberg. We all had to show up for work before seven o'clock in the morning, but I was late once. As punishment, I was forced to wear the penis tie, which was wide at the bottom, with a pair of balls and the head poking up under my chin. I was never late for work again. Everyone from the blue buttons to the bosses had to wear the penis tie if they were late. This for me outlined the ethos of the firm, that everyone had to muck in creating a great team environment. In some ways, Winterfloods was like being in the army, we were highly trained to do our jobs, and we all loved the banter.

Brokers would call the market-makers, commonly known as stock jobbers, on the phone asking for the best prices they could get for the stocks they wanted to buy. We could see what the different market-makers were willing to buy and sell each stock for, and each separate price was lit up on the board. The market makers would read them out over the phone and negotiate the finer details of the price.

That's what I wanted to be, so I worked my way up from a blue button. When I started at Winterfloods we made markets in 200 companies, nearly all of which were smaller UK businesses. As Winterfloods developed, we expanded into the rest of the UK stock market. In 1999, we expanded from the UK into Europe, and I was put in charge of the European market-making business. European stocks had always been tradable, but it was quite difficult to do. We made this easier by quoting prices in Sterling and by giving stockbrokers easy solutions to settle the trades.

The business naturally expanded through competition among the traders in a way that was really cutting edge at the time. The universe of stocks was split between each dealer in alphabetical order. One dealer made markets in stocks with names that started with A and B, another dealer had companies with names starting with C and D, and so on. The reason was that a trader could just get lucky with the sector he or she is running. Usually, there are specialist market makers in those fields. The problem was you could be a good trader and be in the wrong sector. By splitting the world up alphabetically, Winterfloods made the compensation a bit fairer.

That was when I started to think about sectors and why I'm able to invest now -- because I know how to split the world up into sectors. A great sector will give you a big tailwind -- or the exact opposite can happen.

One sector that caught my attention was London's insurance market, Lloyd's, which earned income from insurance premiums but ignored the underlying risk. This led to a disastrous loss of capital over which people literally killed themselves. While I was at Winterfloods, many wealthy people became members of Lloyd's of London, using their own money to fund the insurance market in exchange for a share of its profits. Most people would ask me, "Why wouldn't you become a member?"

My answer was that the members faced unlimited liability. For example, claims for asbestos-related diseases dating back to the 1940s flooded Lloyd's after U.S. courts ruled that anyone who had been exposed to asbestos could file a claim, regardless of whether or not they showed symptoms of illness. The courts could make claims on other assets in your name to cover the liability. Judges, members of Parliament, members of the royal family, sports champions, and even ordinary housewives were bankrupted. Fifteen people committed suicide and more than 500 people filed for bankruptcy.

Everyone I knew at Winterfloods knew someone involved in the Lloyd's scandal. The debacle taught me at an early age that, when it comes to making money, there is never a free lunch. If an opportunity looks too good to be true, it usually is.

Then something very real happened: the internet. Like a lot of other businesses that had looked unsinkable, the market-making business was severely disrupted by technology. Suddenly, brokers could place their own orders on the screen. If they weren't happy with our prices, they could simply undercut us. As the technology advanced, I could see that our margins were under pressure.

Before the internet removed the barriers to entry, only market makers could set prices. Our only competition was the other market-makers, such as UBS and Merrill Lynch. With this new technology, anyone could interact with the market, making the margins only go one way – down.

Just as I did at the age of 14, when I predicted the death of the laundromat business in Liverpool, or while in Milan, when my children laughed at the "beekeepers" in hazmat suits, I saw the way forward when no one around me could. I saw that market makers were about to be driven out of business. Winterfloods is still around, but they all have to work much harder for less profit. It's much less lucrative than it used to be.

Winterfloods had only one securities analyst, Laurence Marsh, who would visit companies when they went public. He gave me a book entitled, "Buffett: The Making of An American Capitalist" by Roger Lowenstein. I loved it. I immediately recognized Warren Buffett as the best investor in the world. I learned quickly from one of Buffett's axioms: "The best advice I have received on investing is that investing is simple but it's not easy because emotions get in people's way, they get all excited about stocks when they've gone up and they get depressed when they've gone down." I think what resonated with me most, and still does today, was how humble Buffett is. He lives in the same house he bought in 1958, though he bought a new Cadillac in 2014. Even today, I think he is a great role model for the whole of society. He has not overcomplicated his life. He has kept it simple and has not been distracted.

Laurence Marsh introduced me to his friend John Horseman, who was starting his own hedge fund. John reminded me in some ways of Buffett -- an incredibly humble and selfless man who kept life simple. A lot of hedge funds had been taken out by the market in 1994, but I could see right away that John was different. I asked him, "What style of investor are you?"

He said, "I just focus on themes and sectors."

My ears pricked up. That was how I had learned to think

about stocks at Winterfloods. It was exactly what I wanted to do. That was the skill set I wanted to develop in myself.

I said, "Can you offer me a job? I want to get into the hedge fund space. I like the way you think."

Chris Harrison worked with John as his CFO. I met them both in a pub in Belgravia, and they offered me the job. I owe a lot to both of them. Looking back, I was a real rookie, and they put a lot of faith in me.

As head of European trading, I left a lot of money behind at Winterfloods. At that time in the City, compensation was paid out over five years, so I walked away from quite a big retainer. Market-making had paid the bills and had given me a standard of living beyond most people my age. However, it was no longer what I wanted to do with my life, and I could see that the internet was going to disrupt the business.

I made the decision that I couldn't be locked into this business forever. I wanted to invest. Everyone I knew thought I was crazy to leave it behind. I had two girls, Annie and Maisie, both below the age of two. Having seen how my father ran his laundromat, I was driven to take the risk and move away from the business. I did not want to make the same mistake my father had.

I told myself, "Either do it now or don't do it at all. Just make the move." I left Winterfloods in 2003 and never looked back.

CHAPTER FOUR: IT DOESN'T TAKE A WIZARD

It wasn't a coincidence that the hottest U.S. growth stocks were the first long positions I took at the outbreak of the COVID-19 pandemic after shorting what might as well have been the rest of the world. As a European equity hedge fund manager entering early retirement at forty-seven, I felt like a kid in a candy store. Finally, I could buy what I wanted. At Horseman Capital, where I had ogled the candy canes and chocolate truffles behind the window, the problem was never that I didn't have enough coins in the piggy bank. It was that my parents wouldn't let me taste the sweets.

Simply put, it had been my mandate as a portfolio manager at Horseman to find the best possible investments in Europe's stock market. Unfortunately, a lot of my energy was consumed by BREXIT and the European debt crisis. Europe had become a backwater for technology companies while the U.S. gained a significant lead. These events turned Europe into a laundromat. Though I was allowed to buy American stocks, running a fund with Europe in the title made it difficult. The longer I stayed at Horseman, the more obvious it became that the ways people made money were changing – and the more I looked to invest in the hot U.S. growth companies that consistently developed new products and services. These are the companies with products that my children and all of their European friends were spending their allowance on, from social media apps and online games to slick phones and game consoles.

That's where the growth is – and will continue to be when my children are fully grown. As adults, they will spend their salaries on products that will use the internet as infrastructure from touchless payment systems that will let them walk out of a store with merchandise -- without even swiping a credit card -- to autonomous cars that will let them watch movies online while driving them to work.

I've seen a lot of books on the shelves written by the Wizards of Wall Street. They'll tell you how to make a fortune in the stock market. But they don't bother to retell the oldest joke on Wall Street: How do you make a million dollars on the stock market? Start out with two million dollars. Well, ignore the man behind the curtain. He's as fake as the Wizard of Oz.

Now even these great wizards are being disrupted by technology. Their ways of making money are now clearly becoming outdated.

What no one tells you is that investing in the stock market is a lot simpler than you think. All you have to do is think of the 10 products that you like the most -- whether or not you can afford to own them – and make sure they are made by public listed companies. One more thing: Make sure young people are now using those products -- and will continue to use them.

What you invariably come up with is a list of hot growth stocks that have four things in common:

- Many aren't profitable enough to fit the criteria for inclusion in the regular spreadsheet.
- They thrived on the technological disruption of the Old Economy.
- They will most likely become generational investments, outperforming major stock markets over a long period of time.
- The COVID-19 pandemic and any subsequent major selloff that guts the stock market should be used as a more affordable entry point.

This is not rocket science. It does not take long to learn how to invest in the stock market this way. It doesn't even require a formal education – as my lack of a university education proves. Don't think that you have to go to university or be a A+ student in math. All you need is an awareness of your surroundings on a daily basis in order to notice current trends and people's habits. It takes me only a week to show anyone how to do this on their own.

For years, I have offered the children of our friends and family the opportunity to spend an informative week at my office in Jersey, an island situated in the English Channel. We call this "work experience" in England — what Americans might call an internship.

One of these promising kids was Oliver. My sister Mandy was his nannie, which is what we call babysitters in Liverpool. I told Oliver what I had told all the others:

- Buy stocks in businesses that you interact with and understand.
- Buy stocks in businesses with products that you like and would be happy to purchase yourself.
- Don't invest in a business where you would not send your own resume.

Oliver came up with a list of publicly listed companies that most boys his age tend to favor. It included Tesla and some gaming stocks -- like Electronic Arts, which produces the legendary FIFA series. All Oliver knew about Tesla was that his dad owned one, it ran on electricity instead of gas, and it cost almost nothing to run. But more importantly, it looked cool -- and he wanted to own one for himself one day.

He had no idea that the electric car manufacturer actually lost $862 million in 2019. That didn't matter, of course. Investors around the world still drove Tesla's share price up 387 percent to $901.00 on February 21 2020, the day before the market crashed, from just $185.16 on May 31, 2019.

I read Oliver's list with a smile and gave it back to him. "There's your portfolio," I said.

Oliver and I have stayed in touch. He texts me occasionally, telling me about a development he has observed in one of the stocks in the portfolio. Oliver's views are more important to me than those of any Wall Street analyst. What I want to instill in an intern's mind is that all they have to do is simply relate the things they do every day with the stocks they pick. Once they make this connection, interns gain a real appetite for following daily stock price moves and news stories as the whole process becomes more real-life. This way of investing and thinking will beat any Wizard of Wall Street.

CHAPTER FIVE: TEAR UP THE SPREADSHEET

Here's the thing. I am a growth investor, but I won't buy growth at any price. I'll buy growth at the right price. That gives me the instinct – an inherent trait, let's say -- of a value investor.

At the same time, I am only buying the equity of companies whose products I expect my children to buy someday. I've never visited a single investor day. I prefer to remain emotionally detached and neutral. I'd rather not take the risk of being distracted by the dog-and-pony show that corporate managers tend to put on for investors. I don't need a corporate executive to look me in the eye and seduce me into buying his company's stock when I can make that decision by finding out if my children or their friends would want to buy its products. So you don't need to visit companies, either.

I don't even try to impose a uniform metric on growth stocks to figure out how much to pay for them. Take Amazon, for example. In some ways, you could argue that Amazon is the biggest online charity in the world. Amazon plows all of its profits straight back into the corporation to develop new products, make its existing products more efficient, and cover costs. Amazon does not return profits to shareholders. This is the textbook example of efficiency as you would see it in an economics textbook in school where profit is described as something that a company shouldn't have if it were truly efficient.

This makes Amazon's business model an aberration in the stock market, where most investors think about how much they can get out of company through a mixture of share buybacks and dividends. Share buybacks reward shareholders as they will own more of the company. It will also boost earnings per share because fewer shares left on the market will mean more profits per share. Most public listed companies also pay out between 30 percent and 50 percent of total earnings in dividends. But Amazon has never bought back any shares, and it does not even pay dividends. Almost no other public listed company operates in this fashion. In other words, Amazon CEO Jeff Bezos is defying the alchemy of the Wizards of Wall Street.

Yet Amazon is destined to keep growing because it is constantly effecting profound changes in the way we all live our lives. Very few of us have ever derived pleasure from driving to a store, sitting in traffic, finding a parking space, walking down endless aisles to find what we're looking for, bumping into to someone you can't be bothered to speak to, and eventually being told it's "out of stock" or – if it is available – finding out that it wasn't what we were looking for. Now, of course, it's just three clicks on your smartphone – and can be delivered to your door almost immediately.

For anyone to have held onto Amazon's stock during its 23-year history of trading on the stock market, they would need to have honestly believed that Bezos was true to his word when he predicted that one day anything and everything could be ordered over the internet and delivered to your door. As of May 5, 2020, enough people had bought into Bezos's business model for the company to be valued at $1.15 trillion, and investors currently pay a fantastically high share price of 116 times earnings. Going forward, the only reason to invest in Amazon is if you believe the company will continue to grow market share over the internet with very little competition.

It's hard to see how any business will ever be able to disrupt Amazon -- even with technology. The more you buy from Amazon, the more it gets to know you -- and the faster it can deliver merchandize to you. Amazon is one of the world's biggest users of artificial intelligence (AI) technology, which allows the company to learn incrementally more about its consumers every second. Amazon sees your buying patterns, what you're browsing, your past purchases, and your customer feedback, allowing it to nudge you into buying more products. By identifying buying patterns, AI allows Amazon to position the most highly desirable merchandise closer to the trucks and withdraw the least sought-after items to the back of the warehouse. This huge competitive advantage is propelling Amazon way ahead of any other online delivery business.

The COVID-19 pandemic has only strengthened Amazon's position against its competitors, handing the online retailer a major victory over companies that had resisted selling their brands on the Amazon platform. They finally succumbed in the Spring of 2020 after municipal governments around the world ordered stores and restaurants to lock their doors, leaving online retailers as the most viable option for any shopper. Unlike the companies that decided to join Bezos rather than beat him, he is willing to forgo profits by spending heavily to keep his myriad global logistics operations running at full speed through the pandemic. As a result, Amazon's sales went up 24 percent during the first quarter, growing faster than they have in four years.

Amazon has always wielded power over the small businesses that generate most of the sales on its site. Now that influence is expanding to include bigger brands that once relied on physical stores for most of their sales. One of the companies that came under Amazon's wing is Geckobrands, which makes waterproof backpacks, coolers and other outdoor accessories. Perpetually reluctant to sell on Amazon, Geckobrands' management had feared that getting cozy with the world's largest online retailer would only alienate the brick-and-mortar stores with which the company was developing relationships. When the pandemic broke out, Geckobrands products were sold in 3,000 locations that shut their doors. Left with absolutely no choice, by May 2020, Geckobrands was selling 50 percent more of its products through Amazon!

For the time being, an overarching need to keep retail dollars flowing in has outweighed a major concern about the ecommerce giant: its creeping monopolization of the global retail marketplace. Before the pandemic, about 45 percent of brands worldwide had refused to sell any of their products on Amazon's website, and more than one-third of these brands said they didn't need Amazon's help to reach customers, according to a survey by Feedvisor, an ecommerce research company in New York that advises merchants who sell their products on Amazon. They were worried that Amazon would squeeze their margins, collect precious customer data, and copy their most-sold products. In response to such concerns, the U.S. Federal Trade Commission started an antitrust investigation in September 2019 by interviewing merchants about their relationship with Amazon. Two months later, Nike stopped selling its latest models of running shoes, apparel and all other products over the website.

To be sure, Amazon still has plenty of market share to take away from its brick-and-mortar rivals. Two decades ago, nobody would have dreamt that Wal-Mart, which has all but eradicated the corner store, could be displaced by a dot-com. Yet Wal-Mart's turnover is still nearly 50 percent more than that of Amazon, which can only mean one thing: There is still plenty of growth left for Amazon.

Even grocery shopping has already been disrupted by Amazon's acquisition of Whole Foods, allowing you to order food online in time for your dinner. Yet the online grocery market is still tiny. In the UK, seven percent of all groceries sold are purchased online. In the U.S, that number is only three percent.

The physicality of shopping has already been disrupted by Amazon Go. This retail platform enables you to walk into a shop, pick up a can of Coke, and walk out without physically paying for it. You'll never have to worry about maintaining six feet of social distance in line for the register, touching potentially contaminated cash, or typing your pin code into a potentially contaminated keypad.

Given the high level of capital expenditure needed to develop Amazon Go and the complexity of the technology, it would be excruciatingly difficult even for a retailer as large as Macy's, which has a market capitalization of $1.7 billion, to develop a competing form of touchless technology in its own stores. So, instead of trying to reverse engineer Amazon Go, they are likely to buy the technology from Amazon. Ultimately, the result for Amazon can only be further growth.

In the same vein, by selling its Amazon Web Service (AWS) to other companies, Amazon will only continue to grow unabated. This secure cloud services platform offers computing power, database storage, content delivery, and other functionality that businesses desperately need to scale up and grow by running web and application servers in the cloud to host dynamic websites. Amazon developed AWS for use inhouse, but it has already sold the technology to other online companies no smaller than Netflix and Expedia. Today, AWS is makes up 13 percent of Amazon's overall revenue -- and more than 70 percent of its overall operating profits. In a charitable way, AWS is funding the rest of the company because its profits never reach shareholders.

Amazon's customers are apparently not discouraged by the company's penchant for raising prices on what it calls a bargain. Amazon now has 150 million prime members around the world, which is a huge step up from the 100 million it announced back in 2018. This is despite the increase in the prime membership fee from $99 to $119 a couple of years ago. Students happily sign up for a six-month "free" subscription before a membership fee appears on their credit cards by the end of the academic year. Prime members accounted for 65 percent of all Amazon shoppers in the quarter ended March 30, 2020. Even though they're paying the difference in monthly fees, they're enjoying fast shipping, streaming movies, "exclusive discounts" at Whole Foods stores, two-hour delivery, and even Amazon Photos.

If there's one piece of advice I would offer any Amazon shareholder, it's this: Hold onto the stock until it's crystal clear that another business has come along with the power to disrupt Amazon technologically. For example, Amazon could get a run for its money from a competitor that develops drones to deliver groceries. However, it's far more likely that Amazon will

31

develop such technology faster and more efficiently than any competitor will. They are always a few steps ahead.

Above all, don't panic when the share price dives. When you think about it, Amazon has been a volatile stock from day one. Ever since its IPO in May 1997, Amazon has fallen more than 20 percent on numerous occasions. Between 2000 and 2001, the stock fell 92 percent. It then took nearly 10 years for Amazon to climb back to the peak it reached in 1999.

Given its current high valuation, combined with the fact that the company returns no profits to shareholders, Amazon can be expected to suffer selloffs of around 25 percent from time to time. I would always use these occasions to ask friends and family if they are still happy with the service provided by Amazon. If so, I would put more Amazon shares in my basket and click BUY.

CHAPTER SIX: THE TIMES SQUARE PRINCIPLE

Another great stock that Wall Street analysts just can't seem to get their arms around is Facebook. They see it as just another website that makes 98 percent of its money from advertising. They're delighted to find a place for the company in their spreadsheets because – unlike many dot-coms – Facebook is actually very profitable. The company's astoundingly fat 34 percent operating profit margin fits quite nicely into their "income" column.

Yet they still treat the stock with disdain, with one finger perpetually hovering over the "sell" recommendation. Their fear is that Facebook's penchant for selling all sorts of personal information about its myriad subscribers to corporate clients who pay handsomely for it will keep landing the company in harm's way.

They are missing the forest for the trees. An easier approach to Facebook is to think of it as a virtual Times Square. Places like that are where you make new friends and businesses convene to exchange goods, services, and ideas. Facebook has taken this concept and magnified it exponentially. That's why I have held onto the stock through thick and thin.

Who would have thought a decade ago that a concept so deeply ingrained in society for as many centuries as a town square could be so easily displaced by technology? Facebook is a digital platform that has the capability to encompass the whole world's population. Just think of how massively huge the actual Times Square would be if it were rebuilt today to accommodate Facebook's 1.73 billion daily active users and 2.6 billion monthly active users, each of whom generates $6.95 in revenue per quarter on average.

As far as I can tell, Facebook has been thoroughly wired for businesses to reach out to the site's users. Take a look around.

Just try to find a company that does not say "Find us on Facebook" on its website. While the older generation still uses the site to re-connect with old friends, it also reaches out to businesses. Facebook has become a business tool.

Facebook owns Instagram and WhatsApp -- social media platforms that are free for everybody to use. Instagram, although used by many businesses, is still more of trendy way for young people to post images and videos online. The younger generation prefers to communicate via Instagram direct messaging. There's more satisfaction to be gained from posting a photo on Instagram than on Facebook. Having a color-coordinated and carefully considered Instagram feed is far more gratifying than posting a picture on your Facebook timeline. You don't see famous football players like David Beckham or celebrity pop singers like Justin Bieber posting pictures on Facebook. They use Instagram to post their latest new single or newly bought football boots.

WhatsApp is a wonderful messaging service that is free. Facebook is looking to monetize it as a way to exchange money. It is developing its Libra currency, which is attracting a lot of attention from regulators who are concerned that it will take power away from governments. This underlines the potential of the platform to displace whole currencies.

Just using Instagram allows you to identify, say, clothing brands that Justin Bieber is wearing. Click on it and buy the clothing directly from the Instagram platform. This is the future of shopping. Thanks to AI technology, there is no reason that anything recognizable by a computer cannot place you on a website to purchase the product.

The pre-eminence of Facebook's virtual Times Square model was put to the test in early 2018, when Facebook's stock price fell by 42 percent. This is when the Cambridge Analytica data breach occurred: 87 million Facebook users' personal data was gathered without their consent by Cambridge Analytica predominately for political advertising. The information gathered was likely to have included the public profiles, page likes, birthdays, current cities and even current locations of subscribers. The data was used by Texas Senator Ted Cruz, who paid $5.8 million for it in 2016. It was also supposedly used in Donald Trump's 2016 presidential campaign to build psychographic profiles based on people's Facebook activity, which allowed Trump to target supporters and potential swing voters.

The data breach was leaked on March 17, 2018, by a former employee of Cambridge Analytica to the New York Times and The Guardian newspapers. Media coverage spiralled out of control with a #Deletefacebook movement trending on Twitter. That hashtag was tweeted almost 400,000 times within a 30-day period after news of the data breach. In 2019, a Netflix documentary about the scandal was entitled, "The Great Hack."

Facebook CEO Mark Zuckerberg responded to the negative media coverage by taking ownership. "It was my mistake, and I'm sorry. I started Facebook, I run it, and I'm responsible for what happened here," he stated.

Zuckerberg faced Congress, and his company paid a $5 billion fine for "violating the law by failing to protect data from third parties, serving ads through the use of phone numbers provided for security, and lying to users that its facial recognition software was turned off by default." In addition, Facebook was required to conduct a privacy review of every new product or service that it develops.

That didn't deter me from holding the stock of course. After all, Facebook's core businesses were still growing rapidly. Even so, it was still hard to make an argument against selling the stock at a time when many investors were predicting that advertisers would boycott the platform and that the business would not survive.

I took refuge on the Greek island of Mykonos to meditate on my losses on Facebook. As I lay on a deck chair by the pool, I noticed a group of women posing in make-up and fancy sundresses for that perfect Instagram-worthy shot. When a couple of waiters approached their poolside table hoisting bottles of champagne over their heads with sparklers protruding from the mouths of the bottles, all the women whipped out their phones and started videoing the waiters with their blazing, flashing bottles overhead. Then they turned around and posed with this extravaganza in the background, posting still more pictures on Instagram. The pool bar and restaurant had posters and signs that said, "Find us on Facebook."

That's when it dawned on me that social media platforms are just as addictive as smoking. Social media is the new addiction of modern times. So why not own the stock?

When I returned to Jersey, I asked friends what they were looking at on their phones. They all said Instagram or WhatsApp. I also noticed that I was receiving fewer and fewer text messages, and all my messages were being sent on the WhatsApp platform. Traditional texting was out of date, and WhatsApp was displacing it. India, WhatsApp's biggest market, now has 400 million users.

It became clear to me that Facebook was not going away – no matter how a big a fine the company had been forced to pay. Convinced that it would bounce back, I used the Cambridge Analytica scandal to buy more Facebook stock at a discount -- just as I would do in the COVID crash of February 2020. Facebook became one of my biggest positions -- and it still is. Sure enough, Facebook's share price soared 75 percent in January 2019.

The physical Times Square may have been deserted by lockdown orders during the COVID-19 pandemic, but Facebook still could take centuries to dislodge from cyberspace. Like Times Square, Facebook will always need to be policed. Whenever I see police on duty on Trafalgar Square or any other public place, I am more likely to hang around for a while with my children and enjoy the sights.

I feel the same way about Facebook. Policing Facebook's social media platform through more regulatory oversight will not only encourage current users to stay but will also entice others to join safely. Any subsequent selloff of Facebook shares due to regulatory issues should be used as a buying opportunity. This cyberspace iteration of Times Squares -- if policed correctly -- will be with us for generations to come.

CHAPTER SEVEN: THE STOCK MARKET IS CHILD'S PLAY

Back to buying growth at the right price, which I did with Amazon and Facebook in March 2020, just make sure you are paying a sensible price -- no matter how excited you are about the company. At the height of the dot-com bubble investors were paying $27 billion for Amazon, which had total revenue in 1999 of just $1.64 billion. So investors were paying 16 times revenue for the stock. Forget profits; Amazon didn't have any. In fact the company incurred $720 million in losses that year. Fast-forward two decades to May 2020, and Amazon trades at only four times revenue. You can argue that Amazon is still too expensive. On the other hand, you can argue that business model has been proven beyond a reasonable doubt. When I made my move on Amazon in March 2020, when the price dipped below $2,000 a share before soaring above $3,000 in July, there wasn't a doubt in my mind.

When you look at investing as simply as I do, anomalies like Amazon become easier to explain to my 13-year-old son Henry than to analysts in the City, the London financial district that we compare with New York's Wall Street. Those analysts spend their days populating spreadsheets with profit margins, expense ratios, earnings forecasts and other minutia, sitting through conference calls with CEOs bragging about how they're trouncing the competition, or visiting factories where they can kick the tires and smudge the glistening surface of a BMW as it rolls off the assembly line. Like most adults in my generation, they just don't feel comfortable investing in things that they can't touch. They shake the instinct.

Adolescents today are much more inclined to see value in the things that they can't touch but are still using every day. That's why they have a tremendous advantage over the majority of adults from my generation. The things adolescents value today are virtual. They operate on the cloud. They're called Instagram, Snapchat, WhatsApp, Animal Crossing, Minecraft, Facebook, Netflix. The list goes on for a long time. The closest they have ever gotten to making physical contact with any of these products is holding an iPhone or a Nintendo Switch in their hands. Our children know far more about these things and what their potential value is than we do. The one thing they don't know – or don't yet appreciate – is that they are all owned and/or operated by public listed companies that they are likely to put on the list of things they like.

As I explained earlier, the obstacle that financial analysts run up against when they try to make sense of these companies is that the numbers they generate just can't be crammed into an ordinary spreadsheet. There is no single metric to analyze each of these stocks and come to the conclusion that they're a "buy" at the ludicrously high prices they fetch on the stock market. But most people just don't care anymore, which is why the share prices just keep rising over the long term. They can see with their own eyes that the products these companies make are hugely successful and will only be more widely used in the decades to come. They've stopped waiting for the Wizards of Wall Street to concoct a rational explanation of how to monetize them. They have started buying the stocks regardless of the lack of profits.

Adolescents are already very far advanced in the process of becoming future investors in the products they're using today. The teenagers who aren't old enough to use them yet talk about the ones they would buy if they could afford them. They might not have a driver's license yet, but they'll talk their parents into buying a Tesla if they can afford one. That's why Tesla CEO Elon Musk has taken out every short seller who predicted that the company wasn't profitable enough to make every capital investment that it has planned. The kids figured this one out long before the adults did.

Anyone born after the advent of the internet is likely to

be much more comfortable investing in something intangible than anyone from my generation. If you want to know what's still going to be producing returns for you in the years or decades to come, just look at how your children choose to spend their time. My daughter Jemima, now 15, watches movies in unison with her friends without bothering to enter a cinema; they just dial into the same Netflix account. My son Henry, now 13, shares moments after rugby games with his friends on Instagram. For the rest of their lives, my children are far more likely to use a credit card than cash because they are going to make many more of their purchases on Amazon than in a physical storefront.

In essence, it's the lifestyle choices of our children that are driving the technological disruption of businesses that most adults probably consider bulletproof. When Oliver gets his driver's license in a few years' time, he's far more likely to buy a Tesla, a car that he will be able to repair with a download from the internet, than a BMW. The one stock Oliver actually bought for his portfolio was Tesla, which was only natural because his father owns a Tesla Model S. Because of his first-hand experience -- and because he has his whole life ahead of him -- Oliver has a firmer grasp of Tesla's real value than the herd of Wall Street analysts who set their price targets for the company based on cash-flow analysis.

COVID-19 only hastened a process that was already well underway. The pandemic has meant that whatever people were already doing, they are now doing more of in response to the pandemic. Anyone who is reluctant to venture out to a department store for fear of getting infected is now more likely make a purchase over the internet than they were during the annual January sale season. You have to remember that cashless transactions were growing rapidly long before anyone in Europe or the U.S. had ever learned to pronounce Wuhan. The irony that it took a global pandemic to seal this deal will be lost on no one for generations to come.

CHAPTER EIGHT: ELECTRIFYING CARS

The corporations that are going to continue growing in the twenty-first century while the oil industry, the gasoline-powered automobile industry, commercial airlines and other value traps wither and die, are the same ones that Wall Street analysts say are too expensive, don't produce enough cash flow, or are run by fantasy-based billionaires. That's why I have to analyze every stock in a different way. What I'm doing is avoiding the next laundromat – that is, any business that is in the process of being disrupted to the point that it's no longer a business you would want to own or be employed by. Mainly, I avoid industries that have been and are being disrupted by technology, and I gravitate toward the companies that are doing the disrupting – such as Amazon or Facebook, as I explained earlier.

As tricky as it is to value the stock of Amazon and Facebook, which are both in services that don't actually produce anything tangible, it can be even more mind-bending to figure out how much to pay for a legacy car manufacturer's shares, such as Ford. At companies where you can literally look under the hood and kick the tires, things get a little more complicated. As it is with internet stocks, the key factor is how successful the company's technology is likely to be going forward.

The definition of successful technology is technology that drives down prices, as it ultimately makes everything more efficient and scalable. Let's look at Tesla Inc., the American electric vehicle (EV) manufacturer. Tesla cars have fewer parts than an ordinary car with a combustion engine, which makes them easier and cheaper to assemble. However, the heart of an EV is its lithium ion battery, which accounted for half of the price of an EV in 2015. Because Tesla is now mass producing these batteries, the price has fallen by 87 percent from $1,100 per kilowatt-hour in 2010 to $156 in 2019. It is anticipated that the price will fall further, to just $100, by 2023, which should slash production costs by somewhere around 40 percent.

All this will lead to the mass production of electric cars, the winner being the company that churns out more EVs per year than any other manufacturer. This will open up new price points for more customers. If I were to place a bet, my money would be on Tesla. Tesla's closest competitors are BMW and Volkswagen, which own Porsche and Audi. The challenge that these legacy leaders face is adding new production lines to their long-established combustion engine factories. Volkswagen estimates development costs at 40 billion euros. It remains to be seen how Volkswagen will self-finance this capital expenditure after paying more than $40 billion to settle the "Dieselgate" gasoline emissions scandal with U.S. regulators. Extracting themselves from this negative vortex will cost such substantial sums of money that very few manufacturers of gasoline-powered cars will survive. The old car industry has no brighter a future than a laundromat.

In sharp contrast, Musk stands out as the modern-day equivalent of Albert Einstein. Just as Musk has found himself in the crosshairs of securities analysts and market regulators, Einstein was a target of the Red Scare witch hunt in the U.S. in the 1950s. I have often wondered, if Albert Einstein was alive today, would I back him as an investor? The iconic scientist was an eccentric character, a bit of a ladies man, a supporter of passivism and civil rights, and far left in his political views. His beliefs drew suspicion from J. Edger Hoover, who actually placed Einstein under the surveillance of the Federal Bureau of Investigation. However, the FBI found nothing on him.

Musk, too, has escaped every attack against him unscathed. In September 2018, the U.S. Justice Department started a criminal investigation into a tweet in which he said he was contemplating taking Tesla private and had secured funding for the deal. Investors claim that Musk misled shareholders through this tweet, and some called it a ploy to squeeze short sellers who have been an irritant for Musk. At the time, Musk was already fighting a lawsuit by British diver Vernon Unsworth, who alleged that Musk had falsely accused him of being "a pedo" in public. I've reached the conclusion that Musk's motive for investing in Space X is to allow him to visit his libelous relatives on Mars!

Like Einstein, Musk is as controversial and eccentric a character as he is a genius of the scientific world. What sets Musk apart from Einstein is that, unlike the Theory of Relativity, you can actually buy shares in Musk's innovative ideas. Can you imagine how far Einstein would have risen as a corporate icon only if only his discoveries had been as easy to monetize as those of, say, Thomas Edison or Alexander Graham Bell?

It's only logical that Tesla has become as controversial as its founder, triggering heated debates across the automotive industry. Hedge fund managers no less famous than David Einhorn of Greenlight Capital have held big short positions in Tesla -- and have been badly burned. Their reason for shorting Tesla is that it is using all of its earned income to aggressively expand its operations while piling up debt. Musk is flooring the accelerator by opening new "Gigafactories" to manufacture lithium-ion batteries in China and Berlin. In just four years, Tesla's interest expense grew from $117 million in 2015 to $641 million a year in 2019, making analysts nervous about the sustainability of its business model. If Tesla doesn't meet its aggressive sales targets of 500,000 cars a year, its operational leverage could drive the business into big losses very quickly.

The problem that investors who are bearish on Tesla will always face is that, simply put, the company makes a high-performance product that almost anyone would want to buy – fully electric cars – and it has had no problem shifting into the manufacturing of new products. As a result, Tesla's revenue has grown from $4 billion in 2015 to over $24 billion in 2019. Like many ambitious CEOs, Musk has been willing to post losses in exchange for growth in market share. So Tesla has racked up nearly $5 billion of losses over the last five years.

BY STEPHEN AND ANNIE ROBERTS

When it comes to investing in Tesla, individual investors who know nothing about the auto industry have an edge over Wall Street analysts who are advising them to sell or short the stock. Those analysts are, of course, auto industry analysts who simply added Tesla, when it went public in 2010, to the list of American carmakers that they already covered -- Ford, Chrysler and General Motors, which have scarcely advanced their antiquated, polluting combustion-engine technology for more than a century. It's ingrained in the psyche of analysts that every single carmaker on earth must achieve an operating margin between five percent and ten percent. If Tesla still can't make a profit from the huge risk Musk is taking on his brand-new electric-engine technology, the analysts' figure, it won't be long before the company goes bust and everyone starts buying gasoline-powered cars again.

What Wall Street has always gotten wrong about Tesla is that it's not a car company. It never has been. Instead, it's a cutting-edge technology business. In addition to electric cars, Tesla also makes Powerwall, Powerpack, and Megapack batteries, as well as solar panels and even solar roof tiles that can power your home. Tesla is also intimately related to the space exploration industry. In April 2020, Tesla revealed in a regulatory filing with the U.S. Securities and Exchange Commission some of the intricate ways in which Tesla works with Musk's other company, SpaceX, which bought $600,000 worth of electric automotive components from Tesla during the first quarter of the year. The filing also revealed that Musk started SpaceX even before he became a board member of Tesla and eventually became its CEO. These facts paint a picture of Tesla – and the ethos behind the corporation -- that is radically different from any carmaker in the world.

Nothing could be more foolish than to use the same metrics that are applied to carmakers to figure out how much to pay for stock issued by a company that is perpetually ahead of the curve in developing new technology. This means auto industry analysts are wrong to presume that Tesla can only gain a five percent or ten percent share of the global car market. Norway, whose government offers generous subsidies for purchases of electric cars, is a far better indicator of the future market share for electric cars. In March 2020, 60 percent of all cars sold in Norway were electric, nearly half of which was comprised of Tesla Model 3 sales.

Another way to estimate the growth of the electric car market is to look at how the retail market has changed since the advent of the internet. Like the conventional automotive industry, the bricks-and-mortar marketplace was made up of myriad participants. When London's High Street went online along with New York's Fifth Avenue, the online retail marketplace was suddenly made up of only a few key players. The biggest is, of course, Amazon, which has over 40 percent of the U.S. online retail market. The second largest – Walmart – is much smaller, with only a five percent market share. The internet had a similarly life-changing impact on the global cellphone industry. At its height, Nokia achieved an operating margin of only 15 percent, compared with Apple's operating margin of 25 percent ten years later in 2020. These dynamics were never predicted by any spreadsheet on Wall Street.

In the years to come, I believe the car market will ultimately be dominated by far fewer key players, which will include Tesla and a handful of legacy car companies, such as General Motors and Volkswagen, that manage to successfully transition to all electric vehicles. As it is with smartphones and online retail, only one player will have a dominant market share.

However, I'm not one to put all of my eggs in one basket. At present, the opportunity to place a bet purely on EVs -- without your investment being diluted into gasoline-powered cars -- is limited only to Tesla. However, if you're not convinced that Tesla will lead the EV industry, or Tesla's share price is too rich for your blood, or Elon Musk's behavior is too unpredictable for your tastes, there's an alternative at your disposal: the commodities market. That's why three percent of my assets are currently in copper and nickel -- even though I still own Tesla stock. While they may not be considered precious today, both of these metals will only grow in demand with the popularity of EVs because they are key components for the lithium-ion batteries that are used to power these cars. Another commodity that is likely to rise in value along with demand for EVs is cobalt. On average, it takes 84 kilograms of copper, 30 kilograms of nickel and 8 kilograms of cobalt to manufacture an EV.

By the end of this decade, the amount of copper used in EVs alone could be equivalent to 18 percent of the known 2017 global supply of that metal. Even more copper will be required to expand the planet's electrical grid and build new charging stations for drivers to recharge their EVs. In addition, the equivalent of 55 percent of the 2017 global supply of Nickel, which is a scarce commodity, could go into EVs by 2030. And these cars could consume the equivalent of 332 percent of the 2017 global cobalt supply, too.

The demand for those metals is rising faster than anyone can dig them up. It takes as long as five years to get a new mine for copper and nickel up and running. This could result in significant spikes in the prices for these metals. You can invest in these commodities by simply buying an Exchange Traded Fund (ETF) that tracks the price performance of these commodities. That's why you should invest not only in the stock market – but also the commodities market – if you really want to cash in on the growing popularity of all-electric cars.

The EV race is on, and Tesla is clearly in the lead.

CHAPTER NINE: AUTONOMOUS CARS

In effect, Musk is building a new type of digital platform that just happens to look like a car. Think of a Tesla EV as a giant iPhone on wheels. Tesla is already producing cars that run on autopilot. Currently, the driver still has to touch the wheel approximately every five minutes while driving under 45 miles per hour on a straight road. But Musk is well on the road to developing a fully autonomous car. While riding aboard this driverless digital platform, passengers will fill their time by playing computer games, watching movies, and surfing the internet. All the time that is now being wasted maneuvering through traffic will be filled in a manner that Tesla will be able to monetize in a whole new way. Just imagine the amount of personal information that Tesla will glean from the billions of hours passengers will spend in its cars using its technology. Tesla will be able to detect new habits and trends that may differ from those visible on your personal computer at the office or your home.

Like Apple, Tesla doesn't just rely on third-party suppliers, making it the master of its own destiny. Apple has recently started using their own processors in their Mac computers instead of chips from Intel, and Elon Musk developed his own proprietary autonomous driving chip instead of relying on AI technology from Nvidia Corp., which develops chips for the automotive market. Nvidia's market capitalization is about equal to Tesla's.

Similarly, the consumer's experience of purchasing a car, servicing it, and repairing it is being disrupted by Tesla. Anyone can purchase a Tesla car as easily as buying a pair of shoes or T-shirt. Simplifying the sales procedure, Teslas are only available in five colors, two standard interior options, and simple autopilot options. Because a Tesla has far fewer moving parts than a gasoline-powered car, it requires less frequent repairs, and the operating system updates itself automatically, just as easily as the apps on your iPhone or Android.

In North America, Tesla is locking customers into its own ecosystem with a network of 1,870 battery charging stations that boast a total of 16,585 superchargers that will add 75 miles of range to a Tesla Model 3's battery in just five minutes. Tesla is taking a page from Apple's playbook. Similarly, Apple ties its iPhone to cloud-based services that customers quickly become dependent upon, including Apple Pay, iCloud, iPhoto, and iTunes. Tesla's market leading network of battery charging stations places it firmly ahead of its competitors, such as Nissan, which produces the Leaf Plus, or Chevrolet, which makes the Bolt EV. Tesla customers will certainly think twice about giving up this habit-forming service. Unlike gas stations, where any vehicle can pull up to any pump, electric charging stations use a specific charger for each car model. Such a network of charging stations would be very hard for conventional automakers to imitate this late in the game.

When Tesla's autopilot software becomes fully autonomous, which Musk has said will happen by the end of 2020, the most immediate beneficiaries will be drivers in rural areas where the strain on Tesla's AI technology will be minimal. Just imagine the difference between making a left turn on Fifth Avenue compared to driving down a straight highway outside Omaha, Nebraska. Autonomous cars will be a boon to anyone living in remote places where driving long distances currently wastes hours of hapless drivers' time every day.

Simply put, autonomous cars will effect many profound changes in our lives. They will allow our roads to become much more efficient. Autonomous trucks will be placed on highways at night to reduce traffic congestion during the day. There will be fewer road accidents, resulting in lower insurance premiums. Insurers will have to build entirely new models around insuring "drivers" who don't actually drive. You'll save the time it now takes to look for parking space because your car will go park itself after dropping you off. Senior citizens will no longer have to rely on younger people to drive them around – or even wait for a bus. People will earn extra income by using their new autonomous cars as "robotaxis" during the long hours that their conventional cars now stand idle outside their homes or offices. Once they have earned a reputation as money-making machines instead of money pits in constant need of gasoline and maintenance, cars will hold their value longer and depreciate less over time.

Obviously, the cost of winning the race to develop the world's first flawlessly autonomous car will be enormously high. Even the mighty Google has gone to outside partners for capital to fund Waymo, its self-driving car venture. In a recent round of financing, Waymo was valued at $30 billion. In the first quarter of 2020, Google racked up losses of $1.12 billion on various investments, one of which was likely to have been Waymo. Cruise, General Motors' self-driving unit, recently had to raise more than $7 billion. Given the very real possibility that the first car to be fully automated could well be a Tesla, investors would do well to stop balking at the company's current valuation of $150 billion. That will look like peanuts for the winner of this race. Like Google's Android operating system for smartphones, the operating system for the first fully autonomous car is likely to become the go-to platform for all cars manufactured in the decades to come.

In my opinion, legacy carmakers don't stand a chance in this race. Even Toyota, which produces the Prius, the most popular hybrid gasoline-electric car on the market, is still being bound to its legacy business of producing combustion cars. All legacy car manufacturers have enormous underfunded pension schemes for workers who have spent more time in retirement than they have worked. Toyota has a $7 billion underfunded pension scheme, and Volkswagen $46 billion at risk in its own underfunded scheme. Any new shareholder, like the Lloyd's of London debacle, inherits this problem. This could be a good reason why the legacy players have been slow to transition to electric cars as any wrong move could quickly put their business cashflows in reverse.

Tesla, the only thoroughbred in this race. Small wonder the company spends next to nothing on advertising while BMW spent $296 million on advertising in 2018 in the US alone.

Players like Tesla are just one reason why the oil and gas industry is dying. The price of alternative energy is dropping fast, thanks to breakthroughs in technology by Tesla and other players.

Another factor I look at is how much of the company its founder owns. No matter what you think of the guy, Elon Musk is so confident in Tesla that he owns over 20 percent of the company. You might shrug that off as just a minority stake, but it's staggeringly high for the founder and CEO of a company that trades on a stock exchange. In addition, Musk maintains control through a super corporate voting structure. Ultimately, this means that Elon Musk is putting his money where his mouth is because he is taking a personal risk in every decision he makes.

The first fully autonomous car will make profound changes to all our lives. This technological advancement could have as big an impact on society as the development of the internet. It is clear that the barriers to entry for developing a fully autonomous car are high, but if these barriers are overcome the rewards will be big.

CHAPTER TEN: THE SPACE RACE

One of the many eventualities that the COVID-19 pandemic precipitated is that the demand for services provided over the internet is growing faster than the telecommunications industry can lay down new fiber-optic cables or build new data centers and transmission towers. Zoom, Skype, Fortnite, Google Classroom, Amazon Go, driverless cars and the myriad necessities of twenty-first century daily life need data to move much faster than it already does. Internet traffic is projected to increase more than 60-fold by 2040. At the same time, limited access to the internet in rural areas, where only 61 percent of the residents have access to broadband, has created a digital divide with cities that enjoy relatively easy access to the internet.

That's why the internet is expanding into space. Space Exploration Technologies, a private company that Musk founded in 2002 to manufacture rockets and spacecraft, had deployed 538 Starlink satellites by June 2020. SpaceX's reusable rocket, Falcon 9, can carry 60 satellites into space at a time. By 2027, Musk aims to deploy nearly 12,000 satellites in three orbital shelves. Following that, he aims to add an additional 30,000 satellites.

In effect, Musk is building the first global utility company. He'll be able to offer internet access to anyone in the world, no matter how rural they are. If he were to build a global fiber-optic network on the surface of the earth or under the oceans, he would come under heavy regulatory scrutiny. However, by launching satellites 373 miles (600 kilometers) above the earth, he is likely to face very little regulatory oversight.

Musk's first mover advantage will make it very difficult for legacy telecommunication businesses to catch up. By the time Project Kuiper, Amazon's orbital satellite startup, is ready to enter the space race, some type of regulatory framework will already have been implemented to mitigate the potential impact of an increasing number of satellites on the night sky. There are already 9,000 objects floating around the earth, only 6,000 of which are currently in use. Musk's launches will triple the number of objects in space over the next five to seven years, which could impact astronomy significantly.

Musk's position today is at least as advantageous as that of Mark Zuckerberg in 2004, when his Harvard University campus social media platform went live with voting contests on which girls looked more attractive in their campus mugshots. Can you imagine the regulatory tsunami that would engulf Zuckerberg if he had started Facebook with a similar stunt in 2020? Thanks to his first-mover advantage, Zuckerberg has successfully thwarted one legal challenge after another, leaving no room for competitors to gain an edge. Similarly, new entrants to the internet satellite industry can expect to face regulatory hurdles too expensive and complex to make the venture worthwhile.

True to form, Musk is staying a step ahead of regulators. His Starlink satellites adjust their orbit orientation to minimize the reflection of sunlight toward the earth, and they are equipped with visors that shield their brightest surfaces from the sun. This will reduce the light pollution produced by satellites, making them less visible to the human eye. In another effort to reduce his impact on astronomy, 95 percent of each satellite will disintegrate -- by design -- when it falls out of orbit.

Musk however, was not the very first player in the internet satellite market. HughesNet Gen5, for example, targets rural areas that are underserved by telecommunication providers. In June 2017, the company had a 60 percent share of the satellite-based residential internet service in the U.S. However, HughesNet satellites are placed at geostationary orbits, adding a round trip of 240 milliseconds to every data package sent -- plus latency by the ground stations that connect them to the internet. As a result, HughesNet subscribers face lags when they play Fortnite or call their parents on Skype.

Every millisecond counts to Musk. This is why SpaceX is taking a different approach by deploying low-orbit satellites, which have to keep moving to remain in orbit. SpaceX's satellites provide much lower latency than geostationary ones, resulting in fewer lags when using the Starlink internet service.

The result is likely to be a mass adoption of SpaceX's new technology. In March 2020, the Federal Communications Commission approved an application by SpaceX to roll out 1 million user terminals in the U.S. This superfast internet service will not only afford an exceptional gaming experience. It will also enable high-frequency stock trading in remote areas where investors once had to call their dealers on the phone.

Project Kuiper is not far behind, thanks to Amazon CEO Jeff Bezos's net worth of $140 billion. Project Kuiper aims to launch 3,236 satellites into a slightly lower orbit than SpaceX's realm at an altitude of 367 miles (590 kilometers) using its own reusable rocket, New Glenn, which was developed by Blue Origin, Amazon's launch business. Project Kuiper is a close competitor of Starlink, as both CEO's are running in the same race with the aim to provide high speed broadband to the entire world, through a series of low-orbit satellites. However, Jeff Bezos is playing catch up to Elon Musk in this industry, with Project Kuiper starting years behind Starlink.

To catch up, Bezos has been selling about $1 billion worth of his equity stake in Amazon every year to invest in Blue Origin, which is privately held. The venture is shrouded in such secrecy that it's still unclear how Blue Origin plans to construct these satellites or even where Project Kuiper's headquarters is located.

What is clear is that Bezos is slowly catching up with Musk in the space race. Bezos is planning to start launching the first Project Kuiper satellites in 2021. He has already signed contracts to launch low-orbit satellites for OneWeb and Telesat.

You need deep pockets to join this race. Musk has spent a

phenomenal $10 billion on his Starlink venture in the hope that revenues will reach $30 billion to $50 billion by 2025. He plans to use the revenues from Starlink to fund a landing on Mars in the hope of creating a "multi-planetary species."

Less lofty goals have driven other players into bankruptcy. OneWeb, for example, filed for bankruptcy in March 2020 – even after it had placed 74 internet satellites in orbit.

The entry of Bezos and Musk into the space race has only raised the stakes for legacy telecom companies, that are scrambling to get their names in the race, but they're not going to get much farther than that. Vodafone, even though its market capitalization of $40 billion makes it one of Europe's largest mobile telecom companies, can hardly afford to compete with the likes of Musk and Bezos because it's shouldering a net debt of $60 billion. So, Vodafone has only one leg in the race, having joined a consortium called AST & Science in Miami, Florida, with several other investors. The investors include Rakuten of Japan, which operates an internet-based shopping mall that bears more than a passing resemblance to Amazon, and Samsung Next, which is the Korean consumer electronics giant's investment arm. By March 2020, the consortium, which created the Spacemobile brand, had invested a mere $128 million – a paltry sum compared with the multi-billion-dollar investments in Blue Origin and SpaceX.

Yet investors are still drawn to companies like Vodafone as safe bets, because they keep paying dividends. Vodafone's current dividend yield is 6.4 percent. AT&T has an even higher dividend yield of 7.35 percent, paying around $15 billion a year, but it's in a similar predicament to Vodafone. AT&T is capitalized at $200 billion, but it's carrying an eye-watering debt of $200 billion.

If they want to become credible competitors in the space race however, these legacy telecom businesses should slash their dividends, otherwise, they will simply fall behind. When it becomes commonplace for a smartphone to pick up an internet signal from a satellite in orbit, the technology of telecom infrastructure will become archaic – and the carrying value of these companies' infrastructure assets will become questionable. Investors have to be aware that these entrenched networks could wind up carrying no internet traffic at all, which would make them worthless. It is difficult to find a major stock market index that doesn't contain a large weighting in telecommunications, so the space race will impact every passive index fund manager in the world.

By building a better internet network hundreds of miles above the reach of regulators, Blue Origin and Starlink now have the potential to dwarf all the old legacy players. There is more than a subtle sense of déjà vu here. The same mobile phone networks that disrupted the fixed-line telephone industry with their cellphone towers in the 1990s are now being disrupted by internet satellites in space! To me, the legacy telecoms business looks like just another laundromat.

That said, we still have to keep our feet firmly planted on the ground while the space race is whirling over our heads. The reason is that we can't buy shares in the companies that are launching internet satellites – not yet, at least. In February 2020, just a few weeks before the COVID-19 outbreak caused panic in Europe and the U.S., SpaceX President and COO Gwynne Shotwell told a group of investors in Miami, "Starlink is the right kind of business that we can go ahead and take public." For the time being, though SpaceX and Project Kuiper are not traded on any stock exchange, and they're not directly owned by Tesla or Amazon. They are the CEO's personal ventures.

So, if individuals like you and I can't buy shares in the myriad new satellites in orbit, how can we make money out of them? All the data bouncing between the satellites, smartphones, self-driving cars and touchless payment systems will ultimately land in the cloud. Everybody has heard of the cloud, but few people really know what it is or -- more importantly -- how to make money out of it. The cloud is basically a sexy way to say, "I am storing my data, in a data center." Until Musk or Bezos figure out how to float data centers in space, they will remain planted on the ground.

There are three ways to make money out of the cloud. The first is to own one of the big cloud companies. The second is to own the chips that go inside the servers in the data centers. The third is to own the businesses that build the data centers.

Gone are the days when every office had a hot and smelly server room brimming with steel boxes and wires and harassed IT engineers stomping in and out. Not only did these rooms present a fire hazard, but it was also a waste of expensive office space, especially in prime business districts. Growing demand for computing power and all its complexities led companies to outsource the storage of data to other companies that specialized in it, freeing up their managers to focus on meeting their actual business objectives. It also allowed companies to expand much more quickly without the need to install more severs and employ expensive IT people to manage them.

These days, it's hard to find a company that isn't outsourcing all of its data functions to the cloud. In fact, not outsourcing would only raise dubious questions.

It's only fitting that the four biggest names in the software business effectively control the cloud: Microsoft, Amazon, Google, and Apple. In China, Alibaba of Hangzhou and TenCent Holdings of Shenzhen are the dominant players. These brands afford an absolute air of trust, and their pockets are deep enough to deliver the cloud dream every business is looking for. If I were running a multinational corporation and Microsoft approached me at the same time as a less well-known data center, I know which one I would hire.

You can tap into the incredibly lucrative cloud business by buying shares in any of these companies. As I explained earlier, Amazon's cloud business, Amazon Web Services (AWS), makes up more than 70 percent of Amazon's operating profits even though it accounts for only 13 percent of the company's revenue. The revenue of Microsoft Azure, Microsoft's cloud subsidiary, grew by a remarkable 59 percent in the first three months of 2020. Because Azure contributes approximately one-third of the corporation's revenue, it's enough to move Microsoft's needle.

Illustrating just how large the cloud is likely to grow in the years to come, Alibaba plans to invest $28 billion in cloud computing infrastructure over the next three years. That's equivalent to half of the company's annual total revenue in 2019. Alibaba is undoubtedly betting that new products like autonomous cars will depend on a seamlessly robust internet network. Alphabet's sale of a stake in Waymo, its autonomous car unit, to private equity investors in March 2020, for example, can only encourage drivers to use their newfound spare time behind the wheel to shop on Amazon, watch Netflix, or Zoom with their loved ones. That logic also helps explain Tesla's intimate cooperation with SpaceX.

The second way to invest in this theme is to buy shares in the companies that make and design the chips that go into the servers. These chips help the data centers process the ever-increasing amount of data swirling around us. The leaders in this field are Nvidia and AMD, both of which are headquartered in Santa Clara, California.

Nvidia is capitalized at $232 billion, making the company almost as large as Disney. Its data center business makes up approximately 30 percent of its total turnover. Nvidia's latest processor performs twenty times better than its predecessor.

At AMD, the data center business is growing furiously. In 2019, the business made up only 15 percent of turnover. By 2023, this figure is expected to be closer to 30 percent.

The third way to invest in the cloud is to buy shares in the companies that build data centers. The top builders are: CenturyLink of Monroe, Louisiana; Equinix of Redwood City, California; and Digital Reality Trust of San Francisco.

When AWS and Azure want a new data center, they don't bother to build it – or even operate it -- themselves. They hire Equinix, which currently operates approximately 90 data centers. The company is capitalized at $60 billion. Equinix shares trade at more than 35 times the company's estimated

2020 profits, making the company's stock more expensive than Microsoft's.

If you want to monetize the growth of the internet – without waiting for Musk or Bezos to take their internet satellite companies public – the safest way is to invest in cloud computing. And the safest way to invest in the cloud is to buy stock in Amazon, Google, Apple, Microsoft, or Alibaba. The companies that make chips and build data centers have much higher valuations, and they operate in a market with lower barriers to entry. As soon as these big cloud computing companies figure out how to manufacture their own chips and build their own data centers, they can be expected to reach into their deep pockets and turn the tables on companies like Nvidia and Equinix.

CHAPTER ELEVEN: THE TOUCHLESS PRINCIPLE

In the Hollywood feature *Mary Poppins,* Michael takes a handful of coins to the bank, where shrewd, serious-looking old bankers offer to compound his money through interest. This classic scene harks back to an era when banks were built like Venetian palaces with fat pillars at the entrance, seducing customers with an irresistible feeling of safety. Hollywood has always portrayed banks with giant vaults overflowing with piles of cash that evoke images of treasure stacked around Tutankhamun's grave. In the movies, however, only the top criminal minds can break into these vaults and get away with the treasure.

Since the financial crisis of 2008, the halo of security that once surrounded the palatial images of banks has dissipated entirely. These days, customers look down on banks as someplace where they could potentially lose all their money or – at best – will only receive negligible interest on their deposits. That's the stigma that my children have associated with banks for as long as they can remember.

But the financial crisis was just the beginning of the end for banks. While they lost a decade begging governments for interest rate cuts and multi-billion-dollar bailouts, laying off tens of thousands of employees, struggling to pass "stress tests," and getting their books back in order, they were technologically disrupted to a deadly extent by the likes of Visa, Mastercard and PayPal. Those companies, and their younger competitors, used the banks' lost decade to build a cybersphere of cashless transactions that circumvent the Greco-Roman facades of Wall Street and the City of London.

Instead of embracing this transformation as an opportunity that has fallen into their laps, shareholders of brick-and-mortar banks from Bank of America to Barclays are still underestimating the impact of what is now called fintech, or financial technology. Convinced that banks will regain their dominance over the global economy if they can just clean up their books once and for all, they still point fingers at the culprits behind the bank failures of 2008 – overpaid CEOs, clueless regulators, hapless ratings agencies, and so on.

The obvious truth that bank shareholders are missing is that the financial institutions that are going to win this game are those that succeed in mining data and anticipating their customers' spending habits most effectively. In many ways, this technology allows banks to get closer to their customers. Companies no smaller than Amazon, Google, Facebook, VISA, PayPal, Mastercard and American Express have instantaneous access to vast stockpiles of data that allow them to monitor consumer and business habits and the latest product trends much clearer than a storefront bank branch. Their digital platforms stockpile every byte of personal data on whatever you buy, the precise location of your purchases, what time of day you spend money, and they run it all through algorithms to map out your buying trend.

Many financial transactions now flow straight through Apple Pay, Amazon Pay or PayPal -- not directly from your bank. That's because big Tech has made payment methods frictionless and easy. Gone are the days where you had to struggle through the migraine-inspiring drudgery of reading a long debit card number, expiry date and security code off your card and typing it into a keyboard when you made a purchase. Long gone are days when you had to cash a paper cheque over the counter. Now PayPal, Amazon Pay and Apple pay allow you to make the same transaction by just entering a password or simply pointing your iPhone at your face. At the end of 2019, there were 441 million Apple Pay users worldwide, and Amazon pay claimed to have 300 million users.

That's just the beginning of a new genre of touchless transactions. Clever app developers are leveraging these new technology platforms to help us all manage our finances better than consumer banks ever did. Gone are the days when you had to spend half an hour standing in line in a drab bank lobby to meet a financial adviser who would saddle you with a package of financial services with an exorbitant commission.

These consumer finance apps, which anyone can download onto a phone or tablet using the App Store or Google Play, actually offer tailor-made financial advice to individuals who don't know how to save and spend wisely. For example, Chime of San Francisco, which has more than 5 million depositors, automatically deposits ten percent of your paycheck in your savings account. Digit, developed by Hello Digit of San Francisco, analyzes your spending habits and automatically saves what it calls "the perfect amount" on a daily basis. Truebill of Washington, D.C., which is funded by venture capital investors including a co-founder of YouTube, automatically cancels subscriptions for services that you don't use anymore.

Teenagers today feel completely disenfranchised by retail banks. When my daughter Annie turned 18, she walked into a National Westminster Bank branch in Jersey. She stood in lines for more than three hours, during which she waited to speak to a teller, who told her to wait to speak with a banker, who told her to speak to another banker. She felt like she was in a hospital emergency room with a sore arm, being told to wait for the nurse to take her vitals, then for the radiologist to take an X-Ray, then for a doctor, then for specialist, and so on. Fed up with waiting, she finally walked out without anyone offering to open an account for her.

On her way home, Annie's friends were amused when they heard that she had even bothered to walk into a bank. It turned out that most of them have never set foot in a bank. "What's the point?" one of them asked her.

So Annie whipped out her iPhone, downloaded an app called Monzo, and opened an account with a few clicks. Even before she received her bright orange plastic Monzo card, which lends a vibrant touch to this otherwise touchless bank's unique brand, she had gained a level of control over her finances that she would never have enjoyed at a retail bank.

Founded in 2015 by Tom Blomfield at the ripe old age of 30, Monzo of London set the record for the quickest crowd-funding campaign in history when it raised £1 million in 96 seconds through the Crowdcube website. The Monzo app bristles with features such as spending budgets, instant spending notifications, loans, Apple Pay, joint accounts, and overdrafts. It even distributes your spare cash into "pots" for savings and bill payments. This touchless banking phenomenon is also developing cool apps for business customers with features like invoicing and integrated accounting.

Blomfield, who did not have a banking background before he founded Monzo, is emblematic of the new crop of digital banking CEOs. The role of a bank CEO has evolved over the last decade from running a domestic bank to serving as a fintech manager to launching and developing a digital banking platform. They are following a parallel track with the evolution of CEOs in the auto industry who, thanks to the development of autonomous cars, are no longer just running automobile assembly plants but are also becoming tech managers with the aim of making the car a digital platform.

The old generation of bank CEOs have lived through hell since the global financial crisis. In Europe, the lucky ones survived the eurozone crisis of 2010. They all had to deal with a heightened level of regulatory oversight. Then they faced a flat yield curve, which was caused by low inflation rates. Inflation had been slowed down by another form of technological disruption: the advent of price comparison websites, which effectively slammed the hammer down on any merchant who tried to raise their prices. The flat yield curve caused their margins on new loans to collapse, turning them into low-return businesses like washing machine manufacturers. Then they had to deal with more severe technological disruption caused by the likes of Apple Pay, which started meting out body blows to the banking industry in 2014.

While traditional bankers on Wall Street might as well have

been wearing horse blinders, the dot-com gurus of Silicon Valley did not miss this opportunity. In 2002, eBay, the online auction site, decided to buy PayPal as its electronic payment platform for $1.5 billion. In the middle of 2015, eBay spun off PayPal in an initial public offering after deciding that it would grow faster if investors did not perceive it as somehow limited by the online auction business. By May 2020, PayPal's market capitalization was $177 billion – nearly six times eBay's valuation of only $30 billion. After the spin-off, PayPal's first CEO was Dan Schulman, who had been running American Express Co.'s online and mobile payment business. For me, this episode showed that digital finance businesses like PayPal can only be developed to their full potential by a CEO with the knowledge of the new online marketplace.

The payment mechanisms that big technology companies are building in Silicon Valley enjoy a tremendous advantage over those of traditional banks. They are built upon huge databases and – thanks to their clever AI technology – they have a superior ability to mine this data. As transactions become easier than ever for the consumer, the money transfer business slips away from banks, and the banks' ability to mine data is weakened.

Now Amazon is dipping its toes into banking by offering small-business loans to companies that sell their products on its website. The tech giant is leveraging a vast stockpile of real-time data on companies that do business over the site, gaining an edge over financial institutions that engage in more traditional banking relationships. Its real-time knowledge allows Amazon to assess whether a borrower is creditworthy based on the data it has on the business. As a lender, the risk to Amazon is not high because it has immediate ability to anticipate demand for a company's products and the issues a company is likely to face with its suppliers. No other lender can match Amazon's proprietary, real-time data on turnover and what's trending online.

In the years to come, any bank that is remotely concerned

about its survival can be expected to approach big tech companies that have demonstrated a superior command over data in order to leverage its capital. Of course, banks with the most advanced fintech will be able to integrate more effectively into big tech platforms. In one example of such a symbiotic relationship, Goldman Sachs joined forces with Apple to issue an Apple-branded credit card in August 2019. Goldman Sachs brings its experience of dealing with financial regulators, weighing the credit risk, and chasing down unpaid debts. Apple brings a strong retail brand and provides Goldman with access to more than 1 billion customers.

By tapping into Apple's platform, Goldman has dramatically expanded its horizon from its bespoke customer base on Wall Street to include 1 billion buyers of computer peripherals and cloud-based services. It would appear that Goldman needs Apple more than Apple needs Goldman. After all, Apple's brand resonates far more than Goldman's.

Against all expectations, the business of moving electronic money around only grew with the COVID-19 pandemic. Many people were afraid to stand in line in a bank behind customers who might not respect social distancing. They were even afraid to use an ATM, which involves not only standing in line but actually touching a pin pad that every other customer has used. At Citibank in New York, for example, the pin pads are on touch-sensitive screens that require you to touch them with a bare finger.

Many people now refuse to handle cash for fear that it could be contaminated because countless people have touched it. It is said that paper money can carry more germs than a household toilet. Even if they're no longer afraid, per se, they are still likely to find the idea of cash unappealing in a post-COVID world. The days when everyone carried a wallet in their pocket or purse look numbered to me. When my own children go out, all they take is a mobile phone.

Investors who never anticipated this touchless principle playing out actually sold down MasterCard's stock, which fell

41 percent in February. The general assumption was that the closure of stores, restaurants, bars and other retail establishments in major cities around the world would give people less of an opportunity to use their credit cards, and that rising unemployment would leave fewer people able to pay their credit card bills.

But I saw it as the perfect opportunity to invest in Mastercard. If you ask most people what Mastercard is, they'll say it's some kind of bank. In fact, Mastercard is a technology business. Its business model is to use technology to link banks and merchants with consumers. The business charges a tiny interchange fee which, with $6.5 trillion flowing through its network last year, adds up fast. Mastercard's annual revenue was up 50 percent over the last three years, reaching $16.8 billion in 2019.

Mastercard's global franchise can only continue to grow with a long-term trend toward online transactions – and our inevitable migration toward a cashless society. In Mastercard's quarterly report in early 2020, they stated that they are continuing their longstanding commitment to financial inclusion and have expanded their pledge to bring a total of 1 billion people and 50 million micro and small businesses into the digital economy by 2025.

Visa, Mastercard's closest competitor, reported a massive payment volume of $8.8 trillion for 2019. That was equivalent to 40 percent of the gross domestic product of U.S. In total, Visa processed 130 billion transactions.

The tailwind that COVID-19 threw behind the credit card business came with the closure of retail stores to walk-in customers. Almost everyone who owned a credit card started using it to shop on Amazon, which owns Whole Foods, or other websites for daily necessities.

It also turned out that unemployment -- a word that tends to scare investors – represented a fast-growing revenue stream for Mastercard. In the U.S., where about 30 million were receiving unemployment benefits as of May 2020, several states offer the option of receiving those benefits by check, direct deposit or in the form of a Mastercard debit card. One of those states is Nevada, where the closure of casinos contributed to the loss of 244,800 jobs in April 2020 and drove up the unemployment rate to 28 percent – higher than any other state in the U.S. Nevada's Department of Employment Training and Rehabilitation issues a Bank of America debit Mastercard emblazoned with a pink bouquet to anyone on the dole who asks for it. Mastercard collects a commission on every purchase made with the debit card, which can also be used to withdraw cash from ATMs.

Another factor likely to have driven up earnings for credit card companies was that addicts of fast-food franchises started ordering deliveries online through Uber Eats, Grubhub or Deliveroo without having to leave the safety of their own homes. On March 27, 2020, McDonald's started promoting 100 percent cashless payments on its delivery service, McDelivery. This was a win for customers who stopped fumbling with money. It also promoted McDonald's as clean and germ-free. It even allowed McDonald's to track delivery payments, leaving no margin for "seepage."

Nevertheless, the cashless trend was already well underway at many establishments before COVID-19 struck. Starbucks, for example, was ahead of the game in testing cashless stores to learn how digital and credit-card payments affect customer behavior. On a recent trip to Canada, I was amazed to see Canadians walk into a Starbucks, pick up their drinks or toasties, and walk out – all within 40 seconds. Starbucks made this possible by developing an app for the iPhone and Android that allows you to order ahead, pick up your drink, and pay without waiting in line. This process limits your contact with people and objects -- and ultimately could lead to increased purchasing. Like Starbucks, McDonald's can see which delivery men or women receive the most generous tips.

For retail businesses, COVID-19 offered a compelling reason to become exclusively cashless while overruling objections from existing customers – and even from lawmakers. In January 2020, the month before public buildings across the U.S.

locked their doors, the New York City Council voted to require stores and restaurants to accept cash for payment on grounds that they had discriminated against customers who lacked bank accounts or credit cards. The American Tex-Mex restaurant chain Dos Toros Taqueria had already gone cashless a year earlier after a couple of its locations had been robbed, co-CEO Leo Kremer told reporters. After making the transition, Dos Toros was never robbed again – and it stopped disciplining employees for cash discrepancies.

Over the next decade, non-cash transactions are expected to grow to the point where they account for ten percent of all financial transactions globally. Not only are more companies doing business online, but more people are increasingly aware of how easy it is to spread germs by handling cash. Sweden is the biggest cashless society in the world, with only 20 percent of retail transactions completed in cash. The UK is far behind, with 42 percent of retail transactions in cash -- about on par with the U.S. For cultural reasons, Japan, Spain and Italy are the world's biggest users of cash.

The final frontier for cashless transactions will be in emerging markets where governments want to make foreign exchange more transparent and shrink the black market. Their motive: increased transparency ultimately leads to increased tax revenue. In India, for example, 72 percent of all consumer transactions take place in cash -- and the black market is believed to be equivalent to half of gross domestic product.

Anywhere in the world, legacy banks that are slow to embrace datamining with AI technology will fall behind. As an investor, I will always look at banks as digital platforms. Of course, it will be a challenge for many of them to rebuild their business models to embrace fintech if they simply lack the knowledge to do so. That's why Silicon Valley companies that are as rich in technological talent as Apple and PayPal, will eat Wall Street's lunch.

The old local branch network model inches closer to death with every dollar that is transferred on the new digital superhighways. Prior to the pandemic, whenever Wells Fargo proudly announced that its 7,400 locations were "serving" customers, I only saw 7,400 locations that it would have to shut down eventually. The financial crisis was a hammer blow to the banking industry, but the digital disruption propelled by COVID will be its death.

CHAPTER TWELVE: THE COVID-19 PRINCIPLE

The COVID-19 pandemic gave a whole genre of companies that had no profits -- and in some cases even losses -- a new lease on life. These companies all had one thing in common: they are all technological disrupters of their respective industries, from RingCentral in office services to Peloton in personal fitness, and they all grew substantially during the COVID-19 pandemic as new customers gravitated toward them over the internet. By May 2020, stock prices for these companies had climbed unimaginably high, having multiplied in value since the companies went public.

Here's the catch. To make money from these stocks, you really have to plug into the dream and be convinced that these were category killers. Only if you're truly convinced, can you hold onto an unprofitable business long enough to appreciate the skill with which it carves out a unique niche for itself in the economy.

Looking back at history, Amazon traded at roughly ten times revenue in 2000 -- the year the NASDAQ crashed, laying waste to the first generation of dot-coms. Amazon, of course, emerged from the ashes, and, as I explained earlier, shareholders still love the company even though they have still never received a single penny of its profit. However, this new crop of companies currently trade at even greater multiples than the dot-coms did at the height of the tech craze two decades ago. There's no guarantee that these companies won't trigger a repeat of the dot-com holocaust -- or that it won't be called "the COVID crash."

There's one thing you can be sure of. If any of these companies show even a tiny hint that they are not performing as well as investors expect them to, their share prices won't just fall 10 percent -- they will fall by at least 50 percent. On the other hand, if they turn out to be a new set of train tracks that can lead the rest of the economy out of the Dark Ages, then they could become the next $500 billion-plus businesses to grace the cover of *Forbes*.

It's up to you whether you want to take this bet. Don't look to the analysts on Wall Street for advice. Again, they simply can't fit these businesses into a spreadsheet -- and they certainly can't come up with a rational evaluation. Nor can they anticipate a market crash for tech stocks with any more accuracy than they predicted the NASDAQ collapse.

Of course, you don't need to invest in any of these companies to bet your future on them, you could just send one of them your resume. Whether they continue to operate independently or their less hip competitors swallow them whole, they clearly represent our future.

Apart from killing hundreds of thousands of people, the main impact of COVID has been to accelerate trends that were already in place. Working from home has made people realize how much time they had been wasting on various forms of drudgery, such as commuting to work. I believe that before COVID, people had refused to accept that there were more efficient ways of carrying out daily tasks. In fact, they were living in a Twenty-First Century Dark Age. As the author James Michener put it, "An age is called dark not because the light fails to shine, but because people refuse to see it."

COVID-19 made us see the light, and I believe there is no going back. I saw the light nearly a decade ago, when I moved to Jersey in 2011. I quickly realized I could carry out my whole job as a hedge fund manager at home, 180 miles across the English Channel from the office in London. All I needed was internet access.

Change happens in our society not only when there is a shortage of something, it happens when something better and more efficient comes along. For example, we aren't using renewable energy because we are running out of oil; we are using it because it has become more cost effective. We didn't move from the horse-and-carriage to the car because there was a shortage of horses; we made this change because the car is a more efficient mode of transportation -- and certainly a more comfortable one.

That is what has happened during the pandemic. More efficient ways of doing things replaced outdated practices. New products and services were tried and tested, and now they are finding permanent places in our lives. COVID-19 forced us to catch up with the times.

Now that you know how much better life can be – assuming you and your family members were spared by devastating COVID-19 -- it is going to be difficult to go back. The question this raises is whether anyone will want to risk infection by commuting to work on an express train or a public bus filled with people now that they have the facilities in place to work from the comfort and safety of their own homes. I think offices will always serve a purpose as many people still prefer working in a shared workspace, and physical interaction is important especially when you're discussing some key decision with your colleagues. But the amount of time we spend in office buildings will definitely decline.

Let's look at RingCentral of Belmont, California, which offers a cloud communication platform that centralizes all of your devices. This business communications solution makes sure you can always be reached, wherever you are. It links companies with their employees and customers via voice, text, HD video, web conferencing, and even fax on multiple devices, from smartphones to tablets to computers. RingCentral offers several packages, allowing any business to choose one that suits its size and the industry in which it operates. The price of each package varies depending on the number of people using it – as many as 999 people if necessary.

Interestingly, RingCentral has its origins in the dot-com boom but still bypassed NASDAQ, the traditional first stop for tech startups. Founded in 1999 and listed on the New York Stock Exchange in 2013, RingCentral had a market capitalization of $22 billion by May 2020. That was on a stock price of 20 times sales, which was double Amazon's valuation before the NASDAQ crash in 2000.

True to its creed, this dot-com is still operating at a loss after all these years. In 2019, RingCentral incurred a loss of $56 million on $900 million in revenue. In 2022, consensus forecasts predict that RingCentral will report an operating income of $200 million on revenue of $1.715 billion.

By 2024, RingCentral's sales are expected to double. RingCentral derives 90 percent of its revenue from subscriptions, which makes it a relatively stable business. All told, 93 percent of its revenue comes from North America.

Simply put, the case for investing in RingCentral is its stock price, which has soared more than 1,000 percent in the last four years. This shows me that investors have absolutely no doubt that the growth of this stock is assured for at least the next five years. The stock market is bellowing, "This is the future! This company makes it ridiculously easy to gather all of your colleagues from the office onto a single website that you can access from your kitchen table!"

That said, before you can buy this stock, you should not only be convinced but actually passionate about the idea that RingCentral is the go-to platform for working at home -- and that it can only grow further, then I would seek employment with this company.

Another business that has brought the office home is DocuSign Agreement Cloud. People used to travel for hours to the office just to sign letters, contracts, affidavits and other documents in the physical presence of their colleagues. Just as email dispensed with the need to sign letters back in the 1990s, DocuSign currently allows people to prepare, customize, send, track and sign legally binding agreements online. In essence, DocuSign has changed the way we do business by removing the physicality of the signature.

This "agreement cloud" allows colleagues, customers, suppliers – and potentially anyone you do business with -- to sign on the dotted line in a faster, friendlier, greener manner at less risk and at lower costs. DocuSign uses AI tools to spot hidden opportunities and risks in an agreement.

People trust this website, and it worked well during the pandemic. That's why DocuSign dominates this niche. According to Forrester Research, "The brand name is now becoming a verb."

Like the other hot stocks in its class, DocuSign is not turning a profit. With a market capitalization of $23 billion, the company's stock trades at 23 times sales. Since its IPO in 2018, the share price had soared 340 percent by May 2020. Shareholders don't seem to mind that DocuSign has reported more than $650 million in losses. The company is forecast to start making a profit in 2021. As is the case with RingCentral, the stock market is completely convinced of this company's growth. While it would take a giant leap of faith for me to climb aboard just yet, I wouldn't mind my children working there.

Another game-changer is Shopify, which has invented what it calls "an easy way to get your business online" by making ecommerce available to the smallest of merchants. The website became a mainstay for retailers that were ordered to shut their doors during the pandemic. They faced a simple choice: Sell your wares online or go out of business.

Even the luddites among retailers have found Shopify easy to use. It gathers all of the ecommerce and point-of-sale features that anyone would need to start, run, and grow their own business onto a single, easy-to-use platform. Shopify promises to help each entrepreneur set up an online store in minutes and bring a new brand to life. The site offers a choice of more than 70 themes with professional-looking templates. Its payments function keeps track of their orders and payments in an easily accessible place.

What investors like about Shopify is that its revenue comes from subscriptions starting at $10 a month per merchant. This revenue is as secure as an annuity. The income is guaranteed because merchants would put themselves out of business if they canceled their subscriptions.

Like other companies that grew rapidly over the internet during the pandemic, Shopify has not earned a profit since its IPO in 2015. In fact, the company's losses exceeded $300 million by May 2020. Capitalized at $90 billion, Shopify trades on the stock market for 50 times sales.

Red ink doesn't phase Shopify's shareholders, though. Since its IPO in 2015, the stock has climbed a staggering 3,000 percent. The consensus forecast is for a profit in 2021.

There is no way of fitting Shopify, RingCentral and DocuSign into a spreadsheet. What is clear about all these opportunities is that they are simply impossible to value with the metrics of conventional equity analysis. If you looked for a price-to-earnings ratio, you wouldn't have found one. If you were waiting for any of these companies to pay dividends, you would still be waiting. Unless you had been willing to bet that their stock prices would continue to climb, you would have missed out.

As I explained earlier, these only make sense as investment opportunities if you believe strongly – even blindly – in their growth. You would have to have an almost dogmatic faith in their ability to continue to generate turnover at any cost and that profits will appear somehow, sometime in the indefinite future.

It takes a little less imagination to see gym clothing brands like Nike, Adidas and Lululemon as solid investments. While I was walking around my house in Jersey during the COVID-19 lockdown, I noticed that my wife and daughters were always wearing comfy yet stylish gym outfits, even if they weren't doing any exercise. I also noticed the increasing number of deliveries arriving at our door from Lululemon, Nike and Adidas.

The convenience and comfort of gym shorts, sweatpants, tank tops and feather-thin T-shirts are clearly the makings of a new bull market. The more time people spent at home during the pandemic, the less worried they became about their appearance, and the more they learned to love the gym-suit look. In effect, the British government promoted daily exercise by allowing people to leave their homes for this specific purpose during the lockdown. Because they were not exhausting themselves with a daily commute to the office, people actually had the time and energy to take advantage of this edict. And welcomed the excuse to leave the house even if they had not previously wanted to exercise. Therefore, they were buying new gym clothes.

Not working from an office, I believe, will create a healthier workforce and a better environment. The time wasted commuting to work can now be repurposed for exercise. This is just another way in which COVID-19 has hastened a trend that was already well underway with an increasing awareness of health through sales of the Apple Watch and Fitbit, for example.

When the pandemic struck, Nike's stock price fell 40 percent while Adidas and Lululemon shares each fell 47 percent. For me, these were irresistible opportunities to buy stocks that I had considered too expensive until late February 2020. At these rock-bottom prices, shares of Lululemon, Nike and Adidas struck me as a good long-term, structural investment

With more people exercising – but still trying to maintain social distance – another company that has done well is Peloton, the online exercycle company. In the future, exercise will be an interactive online experience involving a range of digital technologies. While exercising, you will interact with your environment by listening to music on Spotify, participating in live social media chats, or even ordering a healthy snack on Deliveroo via Alexa, which will be built into your exercycle, treadmill, Stairmaster or rowing machine.

That is the model that Peloton's strategy follows. The wired exercycle or treadmill that you can rent on a monthly basis or buy from Peloton gives you access to thousands of live or on-demand exercise classes on a built-in 22-inch touchscreen. The aim is to recreate the atmosphere and energy of a gym studio in your own home. Professional instructors who run the classes are an indispensable element of the business as their enthusiasm and upbeat personalities keep customers coming back.

Peloton might as well have been designed for social distancing during the pandemic. Many people will never feel comfortable again with the physicality of a gym, where they might be afraid to catch diseases from the sweaty surfaces of exercise equipment. The genius of Peloton's interactivity is that it allows you to work out remotely with friends and even exchange high fives with them online. For further motivation, you can compete with them on the leaderboard. Integrated with Spotify, Peloton lets you preview playlists and save the tracks that you liked hearing in exercise classes.

Investors love Peloton's revenue model, which is secure because it's in the form of monthly subscriptions that include the rental of wired workout equipment. I'm sure most of the subscribers who signed up, because their local gyms were forced to close their doors during the pandemic, will hold onto their Peloton treadmills or bikes now that they have experienced the ease of exercise at home without the risk of infection at a sweaty gym.

However, the development of any business model that is this far ahead of its time comes at a formidable cost. With a market capitalization of $11 billion, Peloton is not expected to make a profit until 2023, according to consensus forecasts. Shareholders don't seem to be worried, though. Since its IPO in September 2019, the stock is up 40 percent.

Another technological disruption that COVID-19 has accelerated is that the way people socialize has changed dramatically. Instead of meeting up at bars and restaurants, they are interacting through social media platforms such as WhatsApp, Instagram, Facebook, Minecraft, and TikTok. Before the pandemic, I had noticed that younger and younger people were now buying the latest iPad or smartphone and immersing themselves in the latest social media craze. Thanks to the ease and accessibility of these platforms, their growth has been off the charts.

TikTok, the app where people upload videos of themselves dancing, was embraced as the cure for cabin fever during the quarantine. With more than 800 million active users worldwide, Tiktok has been downloaded more than 1.5 billion times since the app became available on the iPhone OS and Android devices in markets outside of China in 2017.

TikTok allows users to watch, create, and share short 15-second or 60-second videos with friends and family. If you're lucky, one of your videos gets selected for the For You Page of another user, who might watch it and share it with other users. Whenever my daughter Maisie finds out that one of her videos has landed on someone else's For You Page, she cheers as if she had scored highly on an exam.

The app is so engaging that it's addictive, thanks to the background music, filters and other features that spice up the videos that you produce. The ease of scrolling through videos with one swipe of a finger makes it even more engaging. If you have children, they must have led you through popular dances that famous TikTokers Addison Rae and Charli D'amelio have choreographed.

More people are also listening to music at home, chiefly on Spotify, which now has 286 million users who are active on a monthly basis. Since the pandemic struck, there has been an increase in searches for "chill" and "instrumental" playlists, and more people are listening to podcasts related to wellness and meditation. Twenty percent of Spotify's users were listening to 1 million podcasts on the platform, where podcast content was growing at double digits, in mid-2020. Currently valued at $33 billion, this business, which is based in Stockholm, Sweden, looks like it's driving a structural bull trend.

To obey social distancing rules, the music industry has stopped bands and soloists alike from performing concerts onstage. Because live concerts were the main source of income for musicians, they have had to start performing on gaming websites, such as Minecraft and Fortnite to keep their fans engaged. Minecraft, which was bought by Microsoft in 2014, hosted a music festival on April 25, 2020. About 100,000 people joined the Block by Block West concert on the Minecraft server. What is now a tradition started in February 2019, when Fortnite hosted a concert featuring artists Travis Scott and other artists. Scott's appearance allowed him to launch his new song that went straight to the top of the charts.

This illustrates that even the physicality of going to a concert is going to change now that people can attend music concerts on a gaming server at home. Thanks to this merger of the concert and gaming businesses, artists can now attract not just thousands of viewers at once but millions and millions. Scott performed for 12.3 million fans on Fortnite. To put that into perspective, New York's Shea Stadium has a capacity of 45,000 people, so Scott performed for a crowd that would have filled 273 Shea Stadiums. A physical stadium large enough to accommodate a crowd that size would occupy enough land to build the largest city on earth.

When the share prices of gaming companies collapsed in the first quarter of 2020, it was a fantastic opportunity to buy their stock. The following stocks all fell by about 20 percent: Electronic Arts of Redwood City California, which publishes FIFA and NFL sports games; Take Two Interactive of New York, which has the Grand Theft Auto franchise; Ubisoft of Montreuil, France, which publishes the Tom Clancy's series of first-person shooter games; and Activision Blizzard, which owns the Candy Crush franchise. Their share prices soon recovered as the sales of video game software climbed 55 percent during the pandemic.

By the end of 2019, some of the most popular smartphone games had been developed by TenCent Holdings of Shenzhen, China. TenCent is like a mix of Disney, Facebook and Activision blizzard. Tencent publishes Fortnite, Call of Duty, League of Legends, and other games that are household words. It also owns WeChat, a messaging app with more than 1 billion users, largely in China. TenCent is among the sharpest cutting-edge technology businesses in China, where around 95 percent of its revenue comes from.

Tencent is also among the biggest companies in the world, with a market capitalization of $685 billion. Over the last three years, the company's revenue has nearly doubled. Buying Ten-

Cent would not only give you the ability to buy into China but also the most explosive growth areas of the world's stock market.

None of these gaming companies are attractively priced on the stock market, though. Tencent traded at 52 times earnings in July 2020, when Electronic Arts traded at a more palatable 25 times earnings. In my opinion, all of these businesses are structural winners. If you believe in their long-term growth, they certainly have a strong runway of structural growth ahead.

From where I sit, these companies are like Hollywood movie studios. When a new game flops, the share price falls. However, that's just an opportunity to buy more stock in the knowledge that it's only a matter of time before the company rolls out a phenomenally successful new game that boosts the share price. As gaming platforms host music concerts, they will become even more lucrative.

The overall surge in popularity of social media, gaming, fitness, streaming music and working from home is driving the development of technology that increases our productivity. Sports brands, gaming companies, social media and subscription-based exercise companies all represent long-term themes that have only been accelerated by the COVID-19 pandemic.

CHAPTER THIRTEEN: THE INTERNET OF THINGS

When Jersey went into lockdown, young people were the first to figure out that they could replicate the social experience of the physical entertainment industry online without sacrificing social interaction. As I mentioned previously, my daughter Jemima quickly grew accustomed to making appointments with a group of friends to watch Netflix movies in unison from the safety of their homes on either side of the English Channel. They don't share the popcorn they're individually holding in their laps, but they will eventually be able to share the ability to tell Alexa to pause the movie whenever one of them asks for a bathroom break or has to open the front door to receive an Amazon delivery. In the years to come, they will be rest assured of not running out of butter to put on the popcorn or Diet Coke to wash it down because their smart refrigerators will have reminded them to restock when those staples were running low.

Habits like these, so easily formed during the pandemic, have become so widely accepted that they're not going to disappear. They're supported by the "Internet of Things", or household appliances and computer peripherals that are connected to the internet, and they are becoming fully reliant on faster broadband speeds that are supplied by orbital satellites deployed by SpaceX. Now that COVID-19 has magnified the importance of the internet as integral to the very fiber of our being, we can never stop looking for new inroads to invest in the growth of the internet if we want to survive in the stock market.

The Internet of Things led us to adopt an even greater reliance on the internet than we already had prior to the pandemic. While we learn to avoid touching anything outside the home, everything at home is learning to operate by itself. Appliances that you used to turn on and turn off are actually making decisions for you.

The Internet of Things was already huge long before the pandemic. In fact, it's outnumbering the human race. There are about four times more devices connected to the internet than there were people prior to the pandemic. That's a total of 31 billion computers, smartphones, WIFI routers, and other myriad devices, and companies are manufacturing more of them every day. In 2009, the number of connected devices exceeded the world's human population for the first time.

We can't yet invest in the Internet of Things per se. It's not an investable theme. For the time being, though, be sure not to buy shares in companies whose products or services are not "smart" or somehow connected to the internet. If it doesn't produce such devices or services, any company is certain to be disrupted sooner than you think. You might as well buy a laundromat.

Instead, you should buy shares in companies that are tirelessly developing the software and operating systems that enable the internet to engulf our daily lives one way or another. They're easier to find than you think. You need look no farther than Amazon, Google, and Microsoft, which are rapidly developing their power to control every device in your home through their "home assistants" -- branded Alexa, Google Home, and Connected Life, respectively. Because these smart devices are making it so much easier to stay on top of day-to-day tasks, popular demand for them can only grow.

By mid-2020, Amazon appeared to be ahead of the game. While you're cooking in the kitchen, you can tell Alexa to turn on the sprinklers on your lawn, or even turn up the thermostat. Then there's Amazon's Ring, which is truly transformational. It's a doorbell that is connected to the internet, enabling you to see who's at your door and talk to them even if you aren't home. This is ideal for receiving online deliveries. If Amazon CEO Jeff Bezos has his way, everything in the home will be controlled this way.

It's brilliant ideas like these that are driving the growth of these companies to historic heights. Microsoft, which produces software that is ubiquitous across the vast majority of connected devices that you are likely to find in your home or workplace, is now valued at $1.4 trillion. That's equivalent to the gross domestic product of Australia, a nation of 25 million people.

You need to understand businesses like these if you want to invest in the stock market. They make up a large percentage of the S&P 500, the total market cap of which is larger than the U.S. economy. The total market capitalization of all 500 companies that are constituents of the S&P 500 is 10 percent larger than the GDP of the United States.

If you were to buy an American index fund, you would automatically be placing a big portion of your investment in many of these companies. Amazon, Apple, Facebook, Google and Microsoft make up significant portions of the S&P 500, one of the world's largest stock market indexes. Apple and Microsoft make up a little over 5 percent each, Amazon makes up nearly 4 percent, Google makes up just little over 3 percent and Facebook a little over 2 percent, which means these investments make up nearly 20 percent of the S&P 500 index.

You have to think about the future of these businesses to understand the performance of the S&P 500 – and, ultimately, the growth of the world's economy. Let's start with Microsoft. To give you an idea of this company's potential, I would describe Microsoft as being almost like a railroad business. Just as trains must be built to sit on train tracks, most developers of technology choose to build their software to sit on Microsoft's infrastructure. Microsoft is as integral to my life as toothpaste. I get up in the morning, brush my teeth, and click on Microsoft Outlook to check my email. I doubt that this daily routine will be displaced.

Clearly, all the Microsoft businesses are growing. As more people connect to the internet through multiple devices, Microsoft will only benefit. Also, as people put more data onto the internet, again their cloud business, Microsoft Azure, will only benefit. It should come as no surprise that Microsoft's operating income has doubled during the four years prior to the pandemic, growing from $26 billion in 2016 to $52 billion in 2020.

A lot of this growth has come from the company's cloud computing business, Azure, which advertises its ability to "simplify IoT development and drive digital transformation" for offices. IoT stands for Internet of Things. To give you an idea of how lucrative Azure is, its operating profit margin ballooned from 28 percent in 2016 to 34 percent in 2019. Azure won the Pentagon's $10 billion JEDI cloud computing contract, beating its archrival, Amazon Web Services (AWS), in 2019.

However, Google is beating Microsoft by a long shot on another front. Google's internet search engine, which makes up about 80 percent of Google's business, has become so influential that the third most commonly searched word on Bing.com, which is Microsoft's search engine, is "Google." The search engine's minimalistic screen has a white background, so you don't get distracted by popup ads and news headlines while searching. It loads information much faster than any other search engine, bringing you millions of results in just 0.19 seconds. As a result, it now has an 87.35 percent market share in a world where the average person searches for something on the internet three or four times a day.

The growth of this brilliant company looks assured. Listed as Alphabet on NASDAQ, Google is now valued at $980 billion dollars, and it trades at around 30 times earnings. Since 2017, the share price is up 70 percent, and profits are up 40 percent. The company is sitting on more than $100 billion in cash. Despite the fact that Google does not spend money on advertising, I still manage to hear the word Google at least twice a day.

From its headquarters in Mountain View, California, this company has changed so many lives around the world that it's hard to imagine how we ever lived without it. The suite of apps that its cloud computing business supports -- from its search engine to its email client -- are all unpretentious, user-friendly, and fast. Gmail, which currently has 1.6 billion active users, is the most widely used email service in the world. Google Maps accounts for 13 percent of all Google searches, with more than 1 billion people using the app every month. Google Chrome is dominant in the internet browser market, with an approximately 63 percent market share. By comparison, Apple's Safari browser has a 16 percent market share. The reason people use Chrome is that it's known to be secure.

Google also produces the operating system that runs most of the world's smartphones. Google's Android operating system has an 85 percent market share, with 2 billion active users every month. The competing operating system, Apple IOS, can only run on an iPhone or iPad, which represents a much smaller market. The reason Android is so successful is that Google gives it away to manufacturers.

Google Cloud, Google's cloud computing platform, serves as a place for individuals and companies to build and run their own software, and it uses the internet to connect to their software. All these resources are stored in Google's Data Centers, which are strategically placed around the world.

Building a cloud network is so expensive that most businesses decide to outsource it. A recent survey showed that 84 percent of IT managers are using public cloud infrastructure as opposed to corporate data centers. Amazon, according to a recent report, uses Google Cloud despite owning its own cloud computing platform, Amazon Web Services (AWS). Other companies that are using Google Cloud include, Spotify, Snapchat, Coca-Cola, Domino's Pizza, Sony Music, and Twitter.

The cloud race between AWS, Azure and Google Cloud, all remains quite secretive. Google has not released the number of Google Cloud platform users. What is known is that COVID-19 has provided rocket fuel for these businesses as the work-at-home culture has pushed vast amounts of information into the cloud.

Google Meet has also grown with the pandemic as people

seek to connect with colleagues, friends, and family from home. One reason is that Google made the app free to use. As a result, Google Meet was adding 3 million new users per day as of April 2020. By June 2020, it had 100 million daily active users. By comparison, Microsoft Teams had only 75 million daily active users. However, Zoom had 300 million daily active users.

Not satisfied with saturating your computer and your phone, Google decided to make your TV obsolete in November 2006. That's when the company bought YouTube for $1.65 billion. At the time, commentators said Google had overpaid for YouTube, but now it looks like one of the best consumer tech acquisitions ever made. In 2019, the first year Google disclosed YouTube's revenues, YouTube made up 10 percent of Google's total revenue. As many as 300 hours of video are uploaded to YouTube every second, and 5 billion videos are watched on YouTube every day in as many as 76 different languages.

YouTube is becoming the go to platform to watch TV. Some nights at home, my family and I don't even bother to turn on a pay television channel like Sky or HBO. Instead, we watch a documentary on YouTube for free. Our whole family recently also sat down and watched the SpaceX launch on YouTube. My daughters love watching Jeffree Star, Kylie Jenner or James Charles go through their step-by-step makeup routines.

YouTube is becoming as vital a source of practical information as Google's search engine. Today, whenever I need to research a topic or become fascinated by a certain business, I inevitably turn to YouTube, which provides a wide range of videos on millions of topics. YouTube is effectively the modern-day library. I recently walked in on a plumber fixing our washing machine, and he proudly showed me how he had used YouTube to fix it -- even though that was his profession. When my son Henry wanted to be a magician, he learned all his magic tricks from step-by-step how-to videos on YouTube.

When you think about investing in Google, bear in mind that, as more devices get connected to the internet, more people will use these Google services. YouTube was obviously a major beneficiary of COVID-19 and was certainly used a lot more by my own family at times.

Another way you can invest around the edges of the Internet of Things, is to buy shares in companies that are producing the content that keeps us glued to our screens around the clock. This is how the internet has opened up yet another new market for the way we consume content. Of course, YouTube is not the only website that we're watching as we migrate away from TV, which is also being displaced by streaming entertainment on platforms such as Disney+ and Netflix.

Looking at history, I believe this trend could certainly last for another 50 years – which is as long as the radio and TV lasted before the internet displaced them. Businesses that can create great content and leverage it all on one easy to use platform clearly have decades of growth ahead of them.

Sitting down at a prescribed time of day to watch a show on your sofa is a thing of the past. People now are moving away from watching linear TV, where channels present programs only at particular times on non-portable screens. Instead, they're moving toward video streaming at any time of day in any location. This is also putting pressure on movie theaters because people don't need them to watch newly released movies anymore.

Going forward, the downside risk of any internet-based entertainment company is going to be its legacy connection to the physical world. That's why companies are breaking away from any form of entertainment that is tangible. Instead, they are embracing the virtual world.

Take Netflix, for example. When Netflix started up in 1997, it was a website where you could rent DVDs that you received in the mail. At the time, Netflix was directly competing with Blockbuster, the DVD video rental giant. In 2000, Netflix approached Blockbuster about a partnership, but Blockbuster laughed in its face. Blockbuster turned down on offer to purchase Netflix for just $50 million. Now that Netflix is valued at $194 billion, it can laugh at Blockbuster's corpse. Blockbuster went out of business in 2010.

In 2007, Netflix introduced streaming, which allowed members to instantly watch television shows and movies on their personal computers. In 2010, it became available on iPhones and iPads. By 2016, it was available worldwide. Going forward, Netflix will really benefit from increases in bandwidth and expanded access to the internet as SpaceX deploys low-orbit satellites.

Since 2013, Netflix has been disrupting Hollywood by creating its own content. It has produced hit series such as Tiger King, Ozark, and Stranger Things. It has also produced critically acclaimed movies such as The Irishmen and Roma. During the pandemic, my family watched the story of Joe Exotic and his zoo in the Netflix series Tiger King along with 34 million other viewers.

Now Netflix is taking Bollywood by storm, too. While my family was on a train in the middle of India, I looked over my shoulder to notice that my daughter Maisie was watching a Netflix movie on her iPhone. If it's available here, I thought, it can be accessed almost anywhere.

As a result, India is now Netflix's fastest growing market. Indians binge-watch as a nation at a faster pace than the rest of the world, taking just three days to finish a series compared with an average of four days for the rest of the globe. One Indian man actually watched The SpongeBob Square Pants Movie 171 times during 2017.

While movie theaters suffered, Netflix's sales grew from $6.7 billion in 2015 to $20.1 billion in 2019. Operating income has grown from $305 million to $2.6 billion during this period. It should come as no surprise that the stock price went up 700 percent during this period.

What's even more remarkable is that the number of people employed by Netflix has risen at a much slower rate, from 3,500 people in 2015 to only 8,600 employees in 2019. Unlike most companies, Netflix can keep growing without adding a lot of fixed costs.

Most businesses that grow this quickly employ a lot more people, whereas Netflix doesn't have to. This helps explain the company's skyrocketing profits. Another factor is that the businesses ethos is to treat everyone like adults. Netflix employees are allowed to take as many vacation days as they want -- as long as their work doesn't suffer.

Netflix has amazing operational leverage. When new subscribers join up, the cost of adding them to the platform is minimal. So, each new customer just adds profit. The cost of the content remains the same, whether there's one subscriber or 23 million of them. As Netflix has slowly increased its monthly subscription price, the average revenue per user has risen by 32 percent from $8.15 in 2015 to $10.82 in 2020.

The higher price doesn't deter customers, due to Netflix's great content. Netflix's monthly subscription price is the same price as an average bottle of wine. This shows me that they have the potential to increase prices further. I believe this is good value for money, considering the great service they offer.

Netflix easily has the ability to keep growing for many decades to come. With 182 million paying subscribers worldwide, its potential global market is huge. During the pandemic, Netflix added 15.8 million subscribers -- more than double the 7.2 million that were forecast before COVID.

While the best of the growth in the share price is behind us, I can still think of many reasons to be part of this great company. As long as it produces great content and brings fantastic movies onto its platform, Netflix is assured strong growth. For me, owning this stock is as relaxing and stress-free as lying down on the sofa in the evening and watching a movie on Netflix with a glass of wine.

At the same time, it's clear that Netflix is facing competition from the likes of Disney+, Amazon Prime and Apple TV. Who would have thought that when Blockbuster turned away Netflix in 2000, it would cause Disney to change its strategy in 2019? By 2020, Disney's new streaming service was the only thing holding up its share price after the pandemic emptied out its amusement parks from California to France to Tokyo.

Disney should be a great stock to own over the long term. It created its streaming service, Disney+, in November 2019 to offer all of its movies on one easy-to-use, child-friendly platform. The company has already attracted 54.5 million users by undercutting Netflix with a monthly subscription of only $6.99 per month.

It certainly helps that Disney is known for producing great content, thanks to its acquisitions over the years. Disney bought Lucasfilm from George Lucas in 2012 after George Lucas produced the Stars Wars and Indiana Jones franchises. It also owns Marvel. To date, Avengers Endgame is the highest grossing Disney movie at the global box office, netting nearly $3 billion.

Ironically, Disney's market capitalization at the time of writing is only 30 percent higher than that of Netflix, which shows how little investors think Disney+ is worth. I used the pandemic as an opportunity to buy both Disney and Netflix. While Disney's share price fell 40 percent, Netflix fell by only 23 percent. While investors feared that the closure of Disney's theme parks due to COVID-19 would slash the company's revenue, they were quick to realize that Netflix would benefit from lockdown orders that confined people to their homes.

As a result, I now have a bigger position in Disney than Netflix -- not just because Disney was cheaper but because it has so many more strings to its bow. What investors see as a liability I welcome as a strength. The theme parks business and Disney merchandise are just other ways that Disney can make money. The internet has enabled Disney to stream their movies online and leverage their brand straight into people's homes during the pandemic. While Disney has been slow to put all their movies on one easy-to-use platform, I believe its brands are solid enough to thrive for generations to come. Therefore, this stock is one to hold onto.

There are a few publicly listed companies that make devices that were designed from the start to be controlled by you over the internet. Let's start with Hive of Windsor, England.

Owned by Centrica, which is listed on the London Stock Exchange, Hive is a smart home company with a primary focus on energy saving. Its products range from smart thermostats to smart lights. In recent years, Hive has branched out into smart security, with products such security cameras and motion sensors.

Hive's end goal appears to be a fully connected smart house. Its devices can connect to both Amazon and Google home assistants in addition to being fully programable on a phone or laptop. Hive is very consumer focused.

Then there's Samsung of Korea, which is developing a smart refrigerator. When you run out of milk, eggs, or anything else, the fridge detects that it's missing and either orders the groceries for you online or adds them to your shopping list.

Samsung has also developed a smart plug that makes non-smart devices, such as the lamp on your bedside table, smart. Connected to the internet, this plug enables you to control a lamp from your phone, for example.

A more commercial focus on the Internet of Things has been taken by Honeywell of Charlotte, North Carolina, which has enabled infrastructure to be connected to the internet. This will allow people to locate the source of a leak, for example. The company has installed this technology in planes in order to locate the source of a problem.

Take any angle you can get to invest around the edges of the Internet of Things. The inventors of the early forms of those devices may never have imagined how they would enable the kind of connectivity required to survive a global pandemic. It's hard to predict what form this will take in the years to come, but there's one thing we can be sure of, the Internet of Things will become integral to almost every aspect of our lives -- whether or not you figure out how to invest in it.

CHAPTER FOURTEEN: YOUR HEALTH IS YOUR WEALTH

One of the many trends that was well underway before COVID-19 – and was expedited by the pandemic -- was an increasing awareness of one's health. Significant advancements in technology, from online medical examinations to vegan mock meat, are precipitating a sweeping change in our lifestyles. By mid-2020, when more than half a million people had died of COVID-19 around the world, no louder a message could have been broadcast by survivors than ordering Uber Eats deliveries of the Impossible Whopper from Burger King or the Beyond Chicken Burger from KFC from the safety of their homes. For anyone who was spared infection with COVID-19 – or has recovered from the disease -- a heightened awareness of health and wellbeing will contribute to longer life expectancy.

As an investor, my awareness of this secular trend is growing. Being able to identify not only the opportunities but also the pitfalls is critical to knowing how to make money from it. While there are obvious opportunities in new products that have come to the fore, many pre-pandemic risks still exist. As the strain placed on hospitals continues to drive up the cost of healthcare overall, companies that make products with high sugar content face an increased risk of being taxed by governments -- which could cost you dearly if you happen to own shares in one of those companies.

Among the most obvious investment opportunities to which the pandemic drew attention were advances in the analysis of DNA. We've all heard the insidious rumor that mad scientists concocted the coronavirus in labs to control the population. Thanks to analysis of gene data, this myth was debunked, and the disease was proved to have mutated from bats.

Through a process called whole genome sequencing, scientists have been able to track the transmission route of the virus globally. For example, within a sequence of 39 people in Seattle who had been infected with coronavirus, researchers managed to detect that 35 people had been infected with a strain of coronavirus from China while the other four had been infected by a strain that had come from China via Iran and Europe. This advancement will enable us to trace infections more accurately and determine the best way to control pandemics and manage populations.

Such advances in gene mapping are enabling people to make better lifestyle choices and take preventive measures in order to stay healthy. New methods show clearly if you are susceptible to cancer progression and inherited disorders. They show what medication you should avoid and even show you whether you are better at power-based or endurance-based sporting activities.

As more people become aware that they can prevent diseases before contracting them, they will take the pressure off health services and, ultimately, increase life expectancy. If I had my own DNA analyzed and found out that I was prone to skin cancer, for example, I would certainly spend less time in the sun.

Until recently, a full DNA whole genome sequencing package was very niche. Over the last 10 years, the time and cost of this process has been reduced by a factor of 1 million. Soon it could become as cheap and widely available, and straightforward as a blood test. In the future, you will be able to learn every secret of your DNA, becoming aware of any health risks you face based on your genetic makeup.

At the moment, the problem with full DNA whole genome sequencing is that it takes eight weeks to receive test results, and they are not made available online. You receive a long document in the mail, and genetic counselling is a separate service. The advice you receive from counsellors can be traumatic.

However, when the cost and time involved fall to tolerable levels, the process will become so common that people who don't get their DNA analyzed will be in the minority. Knowing your genetic information will affect your pharmaceutical decisions, lifestyle and dietary choices, disease prevention plans, the human aging process, and life expectancy in general.

One of the pioneers of this technology is Illumina of San Diego, California. Traded on NASDAQ, the company gives investors the opportunity to participate in this massive growth market. Illumina develops and manufactures genetic analysis instruments that look like high-tech microwave ovens, and it also supplies all the consumables, such as kits used for DNA sampling. Capitalized at $50 billion, Illumina enjoys a net operating profit margin of nearly 30 percent.

Certainly, Illumina's stock is expensive, trading at a little over 50 times earnings, but its growth in turnover is assured. Since 2014, the company's turnover has doubled – along with its profits. If you want to get involved in the growth of genome sequencing -- and don't mind paying a lofty valuation -- then Illumina is the stock to own.

One concern that was exacerbated by the pandemic is the risk of picking up an infection if you need to be hospitalized for surgery. The answer is to reduce the recovery time after surgery. Patients who return to their daily lives more quickly after surgery have much higher recovery rates. After bladder surgery, for example, patients used to stay in the hospital for up to twenty-one days, which gave them a 30 percent risk of becoming infected. These days, however, their hospital stay lasts only seven days, reducing the chance of infection significantly.

One of the reasons for this reduced recovery time is a giant leap in medical technology that allows robots to perform minimally invasive operations. These robots are controlled by surgeons with absolute precision. For narrow access urologic surgery, a single incision is made. Instead of recovering from an open operation and being left with a huge scar. Now you're left with a one-centimeter scar, and you're ready to go back to work within a week.

A company that has made giant leaps in this medical technology is Intuitive Surgical of Sunnyvale, California. This $65 billion company is at the forefront of designing, manufacturing, and marketing surgical robots using its da Vinci Robotic System – a pioneer among minimally invasive robotic systems.

While these robots cost more than a million dollars each, the long-term savings for the healthcare industry cannot be underestimated. These machines benefit not only the surgeon and the patient but also the economy. The faster people recover from surgery, the sooner they can return to work.

If you want to tap into the development of medical technology that enables shorter recovery time, don't look any further than Intuitive Surgical. In June 2000, Intuitive Surgical started trading on NASDAQ at just $6.29. In July 2020, it was trading at $580.66.

The desire to avoid getting infected with COVID-19 extends to your general practitioner's office, too. This is a boon to the virtual healthcare market, which has an estimated 1.1 billion users worldwide. This business will really benefit senior citizens, many of whom find it difficult to drive and enjoy the convenience of consulting a doctor from their own home. It will also benefit anyone in rural areas where the nearest hospital can be many miles away and public transportation is sporadic. Ultimately, this industry will improve everyone's livelihoods by making it easier to report even a minor illness to a doctor within minutes of feeling the symptoms.

That's why the business model of Teledoc of Purchase, New York, represents the way forward. This website diagnoses, recommends treatment, and prescribes medication through audio and video consultations with doctors and nurses online. Unlike a doctor's office, Teledoc is open 24/7, and you can easily schedule a consultation with a doctor within minutes from the comfort of your own home.

Since the pandemic struck, virtual consultations have spiked 50 percent at Teledoc. The company reported growth of 108 percent in 2020, with 100,000 visits a week. Rather than return profits to shareholders, the company is plowing the profits straight back into its business in order to keep up with the increase in demand for its virtual healthcare platform. As a result, the company posted a net loss of $98.9 million for 2019. The company expects to start making a profit in 2022.

Of course, old school investors are fixated on profit. If you had waited for Teledoc to make a profit before buying the stock, you would have missed out on a 1,000 percent increase in the share price since the company went public in July 2015.

Teledoc is not the only tech company that sees the role of the general practitioner moving permanently into cyberspace. Zoom is trying to compete with Teledoc with its "Zoom for Healthcare" offering. However, Teledoc enjoys a huge incumbent advantage. Built for healthcare purposes from the beginning, Teledoc has a formidable network of 50,000 doctors. People have more trust in Teledoc's doctors, who have built a reputation for offering proper healthcare advice.

The pandemic also led to a greater dependence on apps that people use to monitor their health, particularly ones that they could rely on during the quarantine. These health apps will lead to longer lives as well as a reduction in diabetes and obesity. They allow you to be aware of your health throughout the entire day, continuously counting your steps and measuring your heart rate. Now there are even sleeping apps that measure the time you spend in deep sleep.

As a result, people's obsession with counting the number of steps they've walked in a day is so overwhelming that it has become a routine topic of conversation. "How many steps have you done?" one of my neighbors asked the other day. Another answered, "Oh, I've reached 10,000!" This craze was inspired by innovative companies like Fitbit, which has recently been acquired by Google.

The Apple Watch and iPhone have an app called Zones for Training. It measures your heart rate, how long you've be exercising, calories burned, and miles run. It also records the times you started and ended.

Under Armour has broken into online fitness with MyFitnessPal, which does everything for you. It logs exercise stats, records calorie intake, and helps you change your habits to meet your personal goals. Once you sign up, you are advised to download Under Armour's free mobile health apps such my Mapmyrunner and a personalized diet profile developed to suit your unique weight-loss goals.

Strava, a great app that my daughters used for their online sports day during the pandemic, allows you to share photos of your activities and follow your friends' exercise regimes. Strava primarily tracks cycling and running exercises. It has a monthly subscription plan.

Another reason people are likely to live longer is their increased awareness of their diet. When it became difficult for many merchants to source fresh meat, poultry and dairy products at the beginning of the pandemic, people who had not already tasted vegan cuisine resorted to trying it. In an unexpected manifestation of tech disruption, vegan brands have improved their recipes to the point where it's nearly impossible to tell the meatless from the meat.

Now many people have converted for life to vegan products made by companies no less mainstream than Unilever and served at restaurant franchises no smaller than Burger King. As a result, global plant-based food sales are set to hit $5 billion by 2020, compared with just $3.1 billion as of July 2020.

When I was younger, vegans were always looked upon as outcasts. Whenever I went to a restaurant there was rarely a vegetarian option on the menu – and never a vegan option. Fast-forward to today, and veganism is actually trendy. In the U.S. alone, there has been a 600 percent increase in people identifying as vegans over the past three years. Now restaurants offer vast vegetarian options – and always vegan options too. Rarely do I see a restaurant menu where the only options are hotdogs, hamburgers, fish and chips, chicken nuggets or curries.

This trend toward a healthy diet comes from people growing concerned over environmental sustainability, long-term health, conservation of domesticated animals, and the global food demand. People have figured out that the production of animal-based food creates twice as much greenhouse gas as plant-based food. In 2015, 4.6 billion animals were raised and slaughtered worldwide purely to provide food. People also want to protect themselves from heart disease, obesity, diabetes and hypertension.

If the pandemic is held at bay, the global population will increase by 2.5 billion by 2050. However, there still won't be enough water to grow the food required to feed them all because 70 percent of the world's freshwater is used for agriculture.

Another reason people are adopting a vegan diet is that they are developing food allergies. According to the Centers for Disease Control and Prevention, there was a 50 percent increase in the prevalence of allergies among children from 1997-2011. In response, people are cutting meat, dairy products and other staples out of their diets to reduce the risk of an allergic reaction.

For an investor in restaurant or supermarket chains, it's important to make sure they always have vegan options. If they don't, they have already fallen behind in a market where veganism is becoming mainstream.

Beyond Meat of El Segundo, California, is driving this trend. It provides food that looks and tastes like meat but is made for a vegan diet. The five building blocks of their mock meat are protein, fat, minerals, carbohydrates and water. They source these building blocks exclusively from plants.

Capitalized at $8 billion, Beyond Meat is certainly a volatile stock. The company's turnover has soared from $32 million in 2017 to $354 million in 2019 -- a tenfold increase. Unlike some tech stocks, Beyond Meat is forecast to start making a profit in 2021. This comes as no surprise to me given that veganism has become so prevalent in the last three years.

Beyond Meat has an edge. It's backed and promoted by icons such as Kevin Hart and Snoop Dogg. However, the stock is expensive, and the company has plenty of competition from the likes of Nestle and Unilever.

Nestle is not about to miss this trend. The company has developed brands like Garden Gourmet in Europe and Sweet Earth Foods of Moss Landing, California. Haagen-Dazs, also owned by Nestle, has launched a series of vegan ice cream flavors. Vegan and non-dairy flavors are among the fastest growing in the global ice cream business.

Unilever has also climbed on the bandwagon, making Hellmann's Vegan Mayo. It also supplies Burger King with the Rebel Whopper, which is 100 percent plant-based. Even McDonald's now has a full vegan meal, having partnered with Orkla Foods Sweden to concoct the McVegan burger.

It's not just people who are trying to preserve their health. It's also the governments on either side of the Atlantic Ocean. Obesity and diabetes continue to place a huge strain on health services. The worldwide prevalence of obesity has nearly tripled since 1975. From 2011 to 2030, losses in gross domestic product due to diabetes are expected to total $1.7 trillion worldwide.

Governments are beginning to take action to tackle this issue by implementing sugar taxes in the hope it will reduce sugar consumption. I'm not sure about you, but I definitely prefer a full fat Coca-Cola to a Coke Zero.

Nevertheless, governments are hoping this will have the same effect as taxing tobacco, which helps reduce tobacco use. According to the World Health Organization, a tax on sugary drinks that would raise retail prices by around 20 percent, would lead to a reduction of consumption of around 20 percent, thus reducing obesity and diabetes. It is estimated that, over 10 years, a tax on sugary drinks of one percent per ounce in the U.S. would result in healthcare cost savings of $17 billion. The savings can be used to promote a healthy lifestyle.

With life expectancy increasing every year, governments need to look for new ways to raise revenue. I believe a sugar tax could be the answer. As an investor, you have to be wary of stocks such as Coca-Cola and Pepsi, as well as companies that promote unhealthy eating. They could be heavily taxed in the future.

Prior to COVID-19, when people were living longer than ever, a main concern was the rise in type 2 diabetes. This came from an increased life expectancy along with increased urbanization, a less active lifestyle, and poorer diets. Since 1990, the number of people living with type 2 diabetes has doubled. If they were all to form a single nation, it would be the third most populous on earth -- with more citizens than the U.S. If current trends continue, one in nine adults will have the disease by 2045.

Diabetes is more lethal than COVID-19. The disease kills 4 million people every year, half of whom are under the age of 60. That's equivalent to one death every eight seconds. It can also lead to amputations and blindness.

If there is a way to try and monetize the nasty threat of diabetes, it's by investing in Novo Nordisk, which is traded in Denmark. The company is one of the world's biggest producers of insulin-based medicine, and it provides low-priced insulin for patients in low-income countries. Since 2010, the company's stock has risen 300 percent. Capitalized at $153 billion, the company has a fantastic operating profit margin of 43 percent.

Another trend toward a healthy lifestyle is the number of people who have quit smoking cigarettes. In 2005, 20 percent of the U.S. population smoked. Today, smokers make up only 13.7 percent of the U.S. population, thanks to an increasing awareness that one in five deaths come from smoking.

As a result, it's getting hard to make a profit from tobacco stocks, which have fallen from their highs in 2017. The share price of Imperial Brands, which owns Rizla, has fallen 65 percent. British American Tobacco, which owns Camel, is down 43 percent. Philip Morris USA, which owns Marlboro, has fallen 38 percent. Some investors are still seduced by their attractive dividends of around 6.5 percent. The way I see it, owning a cigarette stock for the long term would certainly give me a heart attack!

Anyone who was not health conscious before the COVID-19 pandemic has since had a change of heart. There is no question that health care systems have performed extraordinarily well under the significant strain of COVID-19. The worldwide weekly "Clap for Carers" showed how much people appreciated the care that they were receiving during the pandemic and made them more aware of their lack of immortality.

It has become clear to me -- as I'm sure it has to most people -- that we all have a part to play in relieving the stresses we put on our health care systems. Aided by technology and general awareness, the pandemic will no doubt result in healthier living. While 2020 has been all about death, 2021 will be all about life and living longer. If you invest in this theme and look after yourself, health really can be your wealth.

CHAPTER FIFTEEN: THE IMAGE PRINCIPLE

If I were ever forced to reduce my investment portfolio to just two stocks for the rest of my life, I would choose two of the world's most famous brands -- Louis Vuitton and Nike. Although they may appear to have little in common as they represent opposite ends of the retail price scale for wearable goods, both brands are equally aspirational among a fast-growing population of almost fanatically loyal buyers.

Because luxury brands are expensive, buying them gives people a sense of accomplishment. People love to reward themselves for working hard enough to afford a unique product that would otherwise have been beyond their means. The logo adds an exclusivity that can make people feel good even while they're struggling to stay ahead of their credit card bills.

As a result, the steady growth in sales of luxury goods has proved to be unstoppable despite wars, recessions, stock market crashes and – more recently -- the COVID-19 pandemic. A consistent increase in turnover, year after year, has only generated more and more profit, making these companies bullet-proof investments.

Their handsome profits are as predictable as the sun rising in the morning and setting at night. On average, Nike has reported a lavish profit margin of around 12 percent over the last two decades while Louis Vuitton has reported an even higher margin of 20 percent.

No wonder their share prices have only kept climbing over the decades. Nike of Beaverton, Oregon, now trades at $102.71 share, up from an adjusted 17 cents when the company went public in 1980 on the New York Stock Exchange. LVMH Moët Hennessy -- Louis Vuitton, which is the Paris-based conglomerate's breath-exhausting full name, now trades at 404.25 euros, up from an adjusted 27.66 euros in 1998, on Euronext Paris.

The rare occasions when these stocks fall are just opportunities to buy. During the COVID-19 pandemic, Louis Vuitton's share price fell 34 percent and Nike's share price fell 39 percent. I knew they would bounce back up, so I moved right in. In the next recession, they could slide back down again by a similar magnitude, but I would use it as another opportunity to take an even greater stake in these great long-term investments.

I can't envision the day when Louis Vuitton and Nike won't be the brands that almost every adolescent, teenager and twenty-something on earth aspires to own. The riches that these companies bring investors are easily on a par with the aesthetic beauty of their products, from the Nike Dunk SB Low Paris sneakers, which fetch bids of $22,500 a pair online, to the LV crocodile-skin City Steamer satchel, which retails for $55,500. Both businesses provide great quality products that they will always be able to charge a premium for. While not all people relate or agree with the same brands, it is certainly a trend one can't ignore from an investment perspective.

Global brands give people an identity that allows them to stand out in a crowd. A lady walking down Fifth Avenue with a Louis Vuitton handbag slung over her shoulder announces her identity as loudly and clearly as a football fan strutting around in the Liverpool Football Club's bright red jersey or the Dallas Cowboys' blue-and-white jersey. People automatically identify with these brands. Nike became Liverpool's official brand in 2020, putting its logo on the famous red jersey.

The global market for luxury goods has increased from $116 billion in 2000 to $147 billion in 2010 to $280 billion today. Prior to the COVID-19 pandemic, the market was expected to grow by 7.3 percent a year through 2023. Even though Bain & Co. predicted that it would contract by 20 percent to 35 percent in 2020, I still have faith in the power of high-end brands to revive their growth trend. That's why some of the heftiest positions in my old portfolio at Horseman were in the luxury goods business.

What makes these investments truly bulletproof is that the

overall effect of technology on brands -- unlike many businesses, from grocery shopping to travel agencies -- has been more of a godsend than a disruption. Whether they are celebrating a friend's birthday at a bar or attending a Skype conference with their colleagues, people want to be seen wearing their new shirts, handbags or watches.

Brands were made to be shown off. When I was young, some of the local's around my area lived for the sarcasm that would fly whenever they turned up at the pub wearing a new Gucci belt or Louis Vuitton wallet. After the inevitable "ooh," someone would always ask them, jokingly, "Is that fake?" If you're a Scouser, everyone assumes you're too poor to buy anything expensive. They all loved the ribbing, of course, because it drew attention to their luxury purchases. They took turns becoming the center of attention.

Now brands are benefitting tremendously from a trend that was well underway before anyone had ever heard of COVID-19. They were already piggybacking on the viral growth of the internet, where they were increasingly hawking their wares on their own websites, and social media. Adolescents, teenagers and twenty-somethings were going to ever greater lengths to be seen posing at home in their Nike AeroSwift Blue Ribbon Sports tank tops and Gucci Square sunglasses on Instagram, TikTok or Snapchat. As Evan Spiegal, Snapchat's founder, said at a conference in Munich in January 2020, "Social media in its original construct is really about status -- representing who you are, showing people that you're cool, getting 'likes' and comments, those sorts of things."

After the pandemic struck in late February 2020, social media was no longer merely the preferred means of social climbing for young people – it was the *only* method available. Deprived of the privilege of gathering in person, millions of them had all the spare time in the world to shop online, wait for the plain brown packages to arrive at their doorsteps, and take innumerable photos of themselves adorned like Twenty First Century aristocrats, and share them with their thousands of Instagram followers on their iPhone 11s or Samsung Galaxy 5G's. Thanks to the growth of Zoom, it's no longer reassuring to sound confident on audio; they have to look completely comfortable in their wearable luxury on video.

That's how these brands are tapping into a growing population of upwardly mobile young people who are increasingly obsessed with their external image. They're known as the Henry crowd. Of course, I'm not talking about my 13-year-old son here. I'm referring to twenty-somethings who are High Earners but Not Rich Yet. These people have good jobs, and they might take one or two vacations a year even if they don't yet own their own homes. I believe they are the future consumers of the world's greatest brands -- and they are where the growth is.

I would hesitate to call them Millennials or the Gen Z crowd. To put it plainly, I don't bother to read research reports on generational investing that were written by analysts who built their careers by squeezing numbers into cells on spreadsheets. Nor do I want to cram my own investment principles into a box.

Instead, I pay attention to what my own children, their friends, and their friends' friends do in their spare time. Perhaps the starkest difference between my youth and the new generation is that it's now common for young people to be obsessed with perfecting a flawless identity that they are undergoing expensive and often dangerous cosmetic surgery. In their quest for the Kim Kardashian look, people in their early twenties are getting lip fillers and Botox. Women and men alike are now paying big money for the perfect pout on Instagram. They're also paying handsomely to have a string of several tattoos etched across their bodies from head to toe.

This generational trend, which I have watched take shape with my middle-aged eyes, is not going away. It has already become the norm. If anything, the outsiders are the ones without tattoos, lip fillers or Botox.

This heightened importance of image -- thanks to social media -- is an investment idea that you can make money out of. It's not just in luxury brands but also high-end cosmetics companies where the profits are to be made.

Even during the first few weeks of the pandemic, when we were all confined to our homes in observance of lockdown edicts, the first thing I noticed was that many people were still dressing up in fancy clothes -- and putting on layers of makeup -- just to get the perfect Instagram photo or snapchat story.

High-end cosmetics companies like Estée Lauder and L'Oréal are riding this trend to the fullest possible extent. Among their best-selling products are anti-ageing creams, for which customers who are obsessed with how old they look on camera are willing to pay a steep premium. To a lesser extent, Procter and Gamble and Unilever are also beneficiaries of this trend.

Since 2016, the operating income of Estée Lauder, which owns the Tom Ford, Bobbi Brown and MAC makeup brands, has risen by just over 40 percent. As a result, the company's share price has increased by 126 percent during the same period. All told, the company was valued at $72 billion in June 2020.

The share price of L'Oréal, which owns the Lancôme, Garnier, Diesel, Urban Decay and Maybelline cosmetics brands, has risen by 83 percent since 2016. Somewhere between Nike and Louis Vuitton, L'Oreal maintains an operating margin of around 17 percent -- rain or shine. In the financial crisis of 2009, that margin briefly dropped to 12 percent before rebounding.

Because today's consumers can leverage their self-imagery to a greater audience than ever, they now see their purchases of luxury goods as investments that are more worthwhile than ever. This extra impetus to sink disposable income into brands is enabling luxury goods makers to benefit from another boost from technology – in the form of joint ventures with companies in Silicon Valley.

Hermes of Paris, for example, recently formed a joint venture with Apple in which Hermes designs fashionable watchbands and encasements that contain smartwatch technology. Available in "space black" or stainless steel, the Apple Watch Hermes was priced between $1,249 and $1,499 in May 2020.

An intriguing accessory, the Fauve Barénia Leather Double Tour watchband, which wraps twice around the wrist, retails for $489.

This combination of one of the finest brands in luxury with one of the greatest brands in technology makes owning both of these stocks look like a good idea. It also begs the question of how high prices for Apple's products – already among the most expensive in the consumer electronics industry – can climb on Hermes' coattails.

Hermes has managed to climb so high on the price-point ladder that the company now sells the most expensive handbag in the world. Priced at $206,111, the 2015 Himalaya Niloticus Crocodile Birkin 35 carries such exclusivity that you have to be invited to buy it. Then you are taken into a secret room at the back of the store to make the payment -- like making a drug deal with a famous Colombian drug baron. I'm sure the thrill is the same.

The score: Owning this handbag will launch you into the gold standard of social circles. That's why anyone would rather pay for the real thing than a cheap copy from their local market.

Instead of buying that handbag, though, my advice would be to look at Hermes stock. The company's share price has increased by 145 percent since 2016. Hermes' operating margin an astoundingly high 34 percent – among the highest operating margins in the luxury goods business.

Nevertheless, luxury brands have not escaped technological disruption altogether. If the release of the first Apple Watch in 2015 was a boon for Hermes in 2020, it was enough to divert any buyer willing to spend a pretty penny on a watch away from Switzerland, which had been revered as a secretive, impregnable fortress for the watch industry.

The reality is that the Apple Watch was never just a watch. It quickly became the best-selling wearable piece of technology on the market. It combines a phone and a fitness device on your wrist – complete with messaging, apps that monitor your heart rate, and the ability to talk to Siri. Soon the Apple Watch will be able to turn on your washing machine before you get home. This invention essentially created the smartwatch market, of which Apple had 55 percent in June 2020, followed by Samsung at 14 percent.

The impact on Swatch, arguably Switzerland's best-known watchmaker, has been devastating. Between 2015 and 2020, Swatch's share price has fallen 56 percent, and Swatch's turnover has flatlined. Swatch owns Omega, Longines and Tissot, which are among the world's oldest and most famous watchmakers. Swatch also manufactures many of the mechanisms found inside almost any Swiss-made watch.

For me, Swatch was a play on the rise of consumers of luxury goods in China, who buy nearly 40 percent of all luxury goods sold worldwide. Incredibly, there is still room for growth. As China's economy grows, so will the number of millionaires. In 2012, China had only 1 million millionaires, a number that had grown by 58 percent in 2019. That may sound like a lot of millionaires, but they represent only one percent of China's population. By comparison, 6.7 percent of the U.S. population is made up of millionaires.

China drove much of Swatch's growth. From 2010 to 2013, Swatch's stock price doubled, which was enough to convince me that the bet would pay off. Instead, I lost money when the stock fell 70 percent from its peak in 2014.

Like many investors, I had mistaken the smartwatch for a passing fad. I equated the Apple Watch with Fitbit, which was subsequently bought by Google. I never imagined that a smartwatch could replace the sophistication of the Swiss watch. I was wrong.

I was blinded by a sense of confidence that the Swiss watch industry was immune to technological disruption. After all, the industry had survived the Quartz Crisis of the 1970s, when Casio and Seiko of Japan introduced digital watches that were much cheaper and did not need to be wound up. For my tenth birthday, I got a digital Casio watch with a built-in push-button calculator.

The Swiss watch industry fought back with the development of the quartz watch. The battery in a Swiss-made quartz watch lasted for years. The watch never needed to be wound, and it was extremely accurate. When Roger Moore wore a digital Pulsar-brand quartz watch made by Hamilton Watch Co. of Bienne, Switzerland, in *Live and Let Die* in 1973, the message was lost on no one: Swiss watches had retained their status as a traditional symbol of wealth. Then Swatch developed thin watches with funky colored straps at low price points, which seemed to guarantee the Switzerland's share of the global match market.

While there will always be a bespoke market for the Swiss-made watch, it will only ever be a statement piece of jewelry. Think of Jaeger-LeCoultre, where a single technician can spend weeks painstakingly assembling a single Master Control Memovox watch that sells for $15,600. The value of such timepieces grows over time, allowing the original owners to fetch a handsome return on their investment at auctions in Geneva. The mainstay of the Swiss watch industry will be the manufacturing of the inner workings of these mechanical pieces of jewelry. These are the makings of the next laundromat on my list.

One luxury brand that is going against the grain in the car industry is Ferrari, which is possibly the most iconic status symbol in the world. Since the Italian high-performance sports-car maker priced its IPO on the New York Stock Exchange at $52 a share in October 2015, the stock price has soared by 223 percent to $162. The reason is that Ferrari's operating margins increased from 14 percent in 2014 to 24 percent in 2019. Driving the profit growth was an increase in sales of its lowest-priced model, the Portofino, which starts at a mere $214,533, and a new program that allows buyers to select the paint color and other details of their purchase online.

Anyone who can afford a Ferrari views the purchase as a long-term investment. The company builds a little over 8,000 cars a year, making any Ferrari model extremely exclusive. Like buying a Hermes Birkin Bag, you have to be lucky enough to be invited to buy a Ferrari. Car enthusiasts are happy to part with their money, secure in the knowledge that the value of a second-hand Ferrari can only rise. Ferrari holds the mantle for the world's most valuable classic car, the Ferrari 250 GTO, only 39 of which were ever made. Renowned as the top Ferrari model during the 1962 racing season of 1962, a 250 GTO recently sold for $52 million.

The potential disruption to the Ferrari image is the company's plan to roll out quieter, all-electric vehicles after 2025. As the proud owner of a Ferrari California, I can testify that the thrill of the ride is the power of the combustion engine resonating through every inch of the vehicle. The sound that a Ferrari engine makes as the transmission moves through the gears can never be forgotten. This effect could be easily lost when Ferrari, which has already started manufacturing plug-in hybrids, goes ahead with its plan.

Would loyal customers approve of an all-electric Ferrari? If the company's transition to all-electric vehicles happens seamlessly – without ruining its iconic pedigree – buying a Ferrari will always be as solid an investment as a masterpiece signed by Monet or Van Gogh. However, if they fail to make a smooth transition, potential customers -- and even loyal ones -- could be put off.

Of course, technology isn't the only motive for brands to form partnerships. Since high prices actually make brands more attractive, lower-end brands are constantly looking for opportunities to ratchet themselves up a few notches toward the high end. Adidas, once solely a sports brand, has gravitated toward iconic street fashion by aligning with celebrities.

Kanye West, who created the Yeezy streetwear brand, collaborated with Adidas in 2013. Adidas's first Yeezy shoe, the Yeezy boost 750, sold out in 10 minutes after only 9,000 pairs were released in 2015. Customers had to make reservations to buy the shoe online using the Yeezy mobile app. This elite branding exercise made Kanye West a billionaire. The rarer the Yeezy, the higher the value.

The effect on Adidas' stock price was just as powerful. Since

January 2014, the company's stock is up 132 percent – despite a 48.7 percent drop in the stock price at the beginning of the COVID-19 pandemic. Since 2016, Adidas' operating profit margin has risen to 11 percent from just seven percent as of June 2020. If Adidas keeps its brand aspirational, it can keep the profits rolling in. That will make Adidas a good long-term investment.

The problem with making such an aspirational transition is that you just can't rush it. Under Armor learned this lesson the hard way. The brand was being called the "next Nike or Adidas" in October 2015, when the stock price peaked at $51.86. Under Armour's profit margin was close to Nike's, so the claim sounded convincing. The company had been on a roll for five years, driving up annual revenues by nearly 400 percent from a little over $1 billion in 2010 to nearly $4 billion in 2015. During the same period, the share price soared more than 1,400 percent, from just $3.33.

The brand's aggressive growth turned out to be its nemesis. While building its identity, Under Armor's then-CEO Kevin Plank lost control over its inventory growth, which cost the company $200 million to clean up. Then the U.S. Justice Department and the Securities and Exchange Commission investigated the company's accounting practices – like reimbursing employees for "expenses" at strip clubs.

In 2015, I noticed a "40% off" sign hanging over Under Armour's distinctive UA logo at a store. I had certainly never seen a discount sign anywhere near a Louis Vuitton handbag. It was a no brainer that Under Armour's aspirations of becoming a prestige brand were a thing of the past – and that its stock was about to collapse. In June 2020, the stock was 82 percent below its October 2015 high. I did not see this an entry point for the world's next status symbol. The brand has lost its halo.

Ultimately, the test for any brand will be whether China provides a tailwind. The Chinese, always concerned about saving face, are obsessed with their image. They are also obsessed with Western aesthetics – as my children discovered on a family trip to China in 2014. Wherever we went, Chinese people would run up to my children and ask if they could take selfies with them. They ogled the blond hair and big blue eyes of two of my daughters. They even squeezed my son Henry's then-chubby cheeks

When I asked our lovely tour guide why the Chinese were so infatuated by my children, she said, "They're fascinated by the way Westerners look – and there are *four* of them!"

The Chinese are just as infatuated with Western luxury goods, as I've seen with my own eyes on Fifth Avenue in New York and Bond Street in London. They flock to Tiffany's, Louis Vuitton and Gucci boutiques with the same reverence they would bestow upon the Eiffel Tower or the Statue of Liberty.

The perennial fortress for luxury goods is Europe, of course. The continent has an abundance of is luxury brands with a pedigree of craftsmanship and style that has stood the test of time for generations and generations. That's why these iconic luxury brands were in the portfolio of European stocks I managed at Horseman – and they're staying in my family office portfolio.

Kering of Paris owns Gucci, Saint-Laurent, Bottega, Veneta and Alexander McQueen. Listed on Euronext, Kering is owned by Francois-Henri Pinault, who is worth $33 billion. He's the third richest man in France and the 26th richest in the world. By comparison, Phil Knight, who founded Nike, is worth $29.5 billion, according to Bloomberg.

Geneva is home to Compagnie Financière Richemont, which owns Cartier, Dunhill, Montblanc and Chloe. Listed on the SIX Swiss Exchange, Richemont is run by Jonathon Rupert, who is worth a mere $4.9 billion.

Of course, Europe's biggest luxury brand company is LVMH Moët Hennessy -- Louis Vuitton, with brands no less emblematic of haute couture than Tiffany, Bulgari, TAG Heuer and Moet & Chandon Champagne. The group is owned by Bernard Arnault, the third richest man in the world -- with a net worth of $87.2 billion.

Keep your eye on the luxury goods space and wait for an entry point. At the end of the day, what you need to know before buying any of these stocks is just how durable the company's future profit margins are. These companies stay ahead of the curve by charging slightly higher prices for the latest versions of their exclusive products. As long as they continue to be run by strong management teams that know how to keep their products exclusive, luxury goods makers will remain among the world's most profitable companies for the foreseeable future.

CHAPTER SIXTEEN: VICTIMS OF COVID-19

If COVID-19 accelerated the trend toward online shopping, it served as a rocket booster for what had been a slow migration of full-time work from the office to the home. Any company that was capable of allowing its employees to do their jobs from the safety of their own apartments or houses jumped at the chance to reduce the cost of operating its office buildings, particularly in prime business districts like Wall Street and the City of London. As a result, the businesses that have done badly since late February 2020 are likely to have invested heavily in commercial real estate, particularly retail and office space.

Because this trend was well underway prior to the pandemic, it's likely to continue unabated for decades to come. Prior to COVID-19, just 5 percent of workers in the U.S. worked from home fulltime, according to the U.S. Census Bureau. In 2017, a study by Stanford University found that the average worker would accept a pay cut to work from home.

Now that working at home is the norm -- and no longer the exception -- the last investment I would make would be in a company that has any exposure to commercial real estate. I wouldn't touch a property developer, a real estate brokerage or even or a manufacturer that owns office towers where every employee once commuted to work with a smile on their face and a briefcase in hand. The second-to-last investment I would make would be in housing anywhere near the central business district of a major city.

It did not take long for the pandemic to gouge urban real estate values. According to Zumper, housing costs in the San Francisco Bay Area have fallen since the pandemic began. Rents in San Francisco fell 7 percent in April 2020.

In absolute terms, though, living near the headquarters of

a multinational corporation in a big city still costs a huge amount of money. Just ask the employees of companies in Silicon Valley, the San Francisco Bay area and New York City.

COVID-19 has forced businesses to recognize that it's unnecessary for all of their employees to commute to the office as they can work from home instead. This lessens the need for employees to live in the cities where their offices are located. That's why Facebook announced that it is allowing people to work from home permanently if they have positive performance reviews. This has meant that fewer people need to live in the Bay Area. They can move farther away from Facebook's offices in search of cheaper housing.

Of course, moving out to the sticks could come at a price. Facebook, which is known for paying its employees well enough to live in the Bay Area, will undoubtedly be eager to lower salaries at the first sign that its employees are paying less for housing outside of the Bay Area. The company pays a median salary of $250,000, which is linked to the high cost of living in the Bay Area, where a one-bedroom apartment costs $4,000 a month to rent. That's four times the national average.

I'm not saying a decline in property prices has established itself as a long-term trend in cities just yet. However, now that people have the option to work from home, many of them will consider moving out of commuting distance from the office. This trend may also result in companies dividing their headquarters into smaller offices in suburban areas.

The end was already in sight for the commercial district of almost any town in the U.S., the UK or Continental Europe long before the pandemic. COVID-19 has just hastened this trend. Now that everyone is staying inside, most boutiques, restaurants, bars, and coffee shops have almost no reason to open their doors. Like it or not, that picturesque row of storefronts with colorful awnings and flowers in the windows is already a vestige of the past.

If they are going to survive, retail establishments will have to think of new ways to entice customers out of their living rooms. Those that apply technology to improving the dining or shopping experience by making it seamless with limited physicality will survive. When my family and I went into a restaurant recently, instead of being handed a menu, we scanned a code that was placed in the middle of our table, which automatically brought up the menu on our phones. They'll become more pleasant places to be, with less time wasted standing around and complaining about the service. In effect, people will place a higher value on their time after the pandemic. They'll be more aware of how close they are standing to other people in a line – and less patient with inefficient service behind the counter. Fewer customers will be willing to stand in a line for a single cash register operated by a lone laconic clerk while four other registers are unmanned.

This dramatic change in expectations among customers has sent companies no smaller than Starbucks, which was badly affected by COVID-19, back to the drawing board. At its headquarters in Seattle, Washington, the coffee shop chain developed an app that allows customers to order a drink in advance, walk in, pick it up, and pay -- all without waiting in line. This is the kind of technology that every retail store will need to develop if it is to remain in business after the pandemic.

Customers will demand even more improvements before they consider walking into a store rather than shopping online. Stores that don't already have automatic doors will be forced to install them now that people are averse to touching doorknobs, handrails and other surfaces where they can come in contact with coronavirus. Customers will also expect retailers to build in enough space for the requisite six feet of social distance while they're standing in line.

A recent victim of the shift to online shopping is Simon Properties, one of the largest self-managed real estate investment trusts. It develops and manages retail property, including regional malls, outlet centers and community lifestyle centers. Since 2019, Simon's share price has fallen more than 70 percent. Simon's market capitalization is $18.7 billion, but it has around

$25 billion of debt. This illustrates that the long-term trend for the retail business – and the commercial property companies that are so heavily vested in it – can only decline.

In commercial office space, investors who bought office blocks where the rents were tied to inflation rates are quickly finding out that they will no longer receive the steady income that they thought was guaranteed. These investors apparently thought office towers would provide an annuity stream like gas pipelines and utility companies. This mentality has always made people overconfident and led them to pile on too much debt.

COVID-19 was a reality check for anyone who was taught that commercial rents could only rise since the Second World War. Yesterday's business model is being severely disrupted by the technology of the laptop and the WIFI router. Even before COVID-19 accelerated the trend toward working from home, companies had learned to use less office space by allowing employees to come in less frequently and share their desks when they were out.

Over the next decade, I believe commercial property values could fall 30 percent, especially around office blocks. Anyone who owns commercial real estate could suffer some real losses as banks that fund them and investors head for the exits.

Concurrently, I believe residential property prices will come back into balance relative to incomes over the next 10 years, making urban homes much more affordable. This could make it much less challenging for millennials to invest in the housing market, especially in major cities. Millennials will benefit from an increased supply of residential property as older people flee the cities to work at home, online shopping drives stores out of business, and the stores are converted into housing.

The only winners of the commercial real estate game will be those who stayed out of it. They will have invested in intangible businesses like technology that have very few fixed assets. In Jersey, I have noticed that all the new wealthy entrepreneurs who are moving to the island are in businesses that are related to technology. In contrast, the last wave of wealthy migrants were all the big property guys. What this indicates to me is that asset-heavy businesses are clearly in a bear trend. If it's tangible, it's toast.

CHAPTER SEVENTEEN: THE TICKER SHOCK

I've already explained why I've loaded up on hot U.S. growth stocks, but that doesn't mean that a stock is golden just because it uses the internet as infrastructure. It could simply be too expensive. Look at Zoom Video Communications, which, as I've just mentioned, became a huge internet phenomenon during the COVID-19 pandemic, more than doubling its stock price in 2020. Assuming that Zoom's growth is assured because millions of people have started working, exercising and socializing from the safety of their own homes, investors are paying more than 70 times Zoom's revenue for the stock. Despite the fact that 300 million people participate in video meetings on Zoom every day, Zoom is fighting a turf war against larger competitors with deeper pockets. Microsoft's Skype and Teams, Facebook's Messenger Call, and Google's Meet could easily afford to offer endless video conferencing for free without even requiring users to subscribe to their already established online platforms. The chances of Zoom winning that battle by charging users for a monthly subscription to talk in a chat room for longer than 40 minutes – the first 40 minutes is already free on Zoom – are negligible at best. Yet the love affair with Zoom Video Communications has been so blind that a completely unrelated company that trades on the Nasdaq exchange in New York under the name Zoom Technologies was suspended after its share price soared by nearly 1,000 percent because investors were mistakenly buying the wrong stock. This shows me how overexcited some investors are getting over Zoom.

Just because a stock piques your senses, it doesn't mean you should bet against the odds on it. A case in point is Canopy Growth Corp. of Smith Falls, Ontario, better known by its catchy ticker, WEED. This ambitious, seven-year-old cannabis producer owes its success largely to the California State Legislature, which passed the Control, Regulate and Tax Adult Use of Marijuana Act after a majority of Californians voted for it 2016. By legalizing the growth and sale of cannabis for recreational use more than 20 years after the state legalized the use of medical marijuana, Proposition 64 made a state with 39 million people the largest government-sanctioned marijuana market in the U.S. It's also one of the largest in the world, according to advisors to the state legislature. Reaching nearly $3 billion in 2019, legal sales of marijuana in California are higher than in any country in the world – even Germany, which spends more than most countries on medical marijuana. In 2019, medical insurers in Germany reimbursed patients for 123 million euros (about $136 million) for medical marijuana prescription – equivalent to just over four percent of legal sales in California.

While such staggering numbers help to explain the euphoria that has propelled Canopy's share price to astronomical heights, you would have to be on drugs to buy the stock. The stock price reached 36 Canadian dollars a share in 2017, after soaring by more than 250 percent that year, peaking at around 73 Canadian dollars a share in October 2018. That number alone allowed all those brilliant, university-educated analysts on Wall Street to value the whole company at approximately $20 billion, which fit neatly into a box on their professional-looking spreadsheets.

What never did fit into the spreadsheet was that the phenomenon driving up Canopy's stock price was nothing more than a blind craze that hooked investors who were desperate to see a theme. Put simply, the theme was that the legalization of cannabis would definitely increase consumption. Like horses wearing blinders, they could not see the obvious: If you can easily grow it legally on your windowsill from a few seeds in your stash, why would you take money out of your pocket to buy weed from a licensed retailer? In fact, the value of any illicit substance can only fall after it's no longer against the law to sell it. It's only natural that street prices for black-market pot in California are falling to remain competitive with over-the-counter prices. It comes as no surprise to me that Canopy has grown 115,000 kilograms more than it has sold since the end of 2017.

Now that reality has set in, Canopy's stock price has fallen more than 70 percent from its peak. The company laid off 200 people in Canada, the U.S. and the UK in April 2020. Investors are finally figuring out that, in addition to having bought into a childishly naïve theme, they have been diluted like dishwater. Canopy has repeatedly issued new stock, raising the number of shares outstanding to 350.8 million as of May 2020 from 98.5 million in December 2015. Yet the company doesn't even earn a profit. Canopy's operating losses have gone from $82 million in 2018 to $1.669 billion in 2020. According to current forecasts, the company will keep racking up losses until 2024.

All else being equal, the logical choice for me would have been to short Canopy's stock. However, so many other hedge fund managers were shorting the stock, eventually making it prohibitively expensive to borrow. The lucky investors who had shorted Canopy near the peak obviously made high returns.

Investors who bought into this new growth area were willing to pay any price for the stock without understanding the market dynamics. They were ultimately getting too excited about the new market. These investors in Zoom and Canopy remind me that there are still many people who try to pick up nickels in front of steamrollers, but I'll never be one of them. And neither should you.

CHAPTER EIGHTEEN: THE GRETA PRINCIPLE

As an investor, I'll never embark on a crusade to save the planet. Rather, I am looking to gain a handsome return from the stock market and take care of my family. If the oil and gas industry looked like a more attractive investment than renewable energy, I would be the first to buy shares of Royal Dutch Shell or ExxonMobil despite the fact that Big Oil has been blamed for the disastrous effects of climate change.

Yet I can easily identify with the world's most feared environmental crusader -- Greta Thunberg, the seventeen-year-old environmental activist who dishes out straight talk to world leaders at the United Nations. Like her, I was born with a disability that everyone assumes would prevent me from making logical sense of the world -- much less making an impact on it. While I was born dyslexic, Greta suffers from obsessive compulsive disorder, Asperger syndrome, and selective mutism. Like my own children and the interns who have worked at my office in Jersey, Greta is among the many teenagers whose behavior has led me to a conclusion that now seems ridiculously obvious – but Wall Street analysts still can't factor into their spreadsheets.

I call it the Greta Principle. If a company is doing anything that Greta would throw a tantrum over, then don't buy its stock. If you're already a shareholder, just sell it before the mob turns on you with stones in hand.

Thanks to the prevalence of social media, Greta represents a technological disruption to the way millions of investors have grown accustomed to managing trillions of dollars every day. With phenomenal rapidity, her angelically framed adolescent visage spreads across millions of iPhone, iPad and Android screens around the world within an instant of her making almost any remark about how corporations are destroying the environment, whether she's in front of a school or at the United Nations. It's hardly a coincidence that Facebook, Twitter and Instagram were already forces to be reckoned with by the time Greta was eight years old and she fell into a deep depression over the degradation of the environment. Even before reaching the age where she can legally invest in the stock market, Greta has emerged as an entirely new force that investors ignore at their own peril. While 4.1 million Twitter followers eagerly anticipate every syllable that her dainty fingers tap out on her phone, fully grown managers of pension funds from New York to London to Tokyo stand to lose billions of dollars if they don't heed her edicts to the letter.

As a result, large petroleum companies and consumer heavy weights like Coca-Cola and Wells Fargo have become landmines just waiting for unsuspecting stockholders to step on. Ultimately, Greta will force governments and businesses to become more environmentally sustainable and emit less carbon. Every time Greta speaks in public or posts a comment on social media, I pay very close attention, particularly when she names publicly listed companies.

"We are in the beginning of a mass extinction, and all you can talk about is money and fairytales of eternal economic growth," she warned world leaders in a searing speech at the 2019 UN climate action summit in New York.

Heads of state who grew up in a carbon-emitting world are fighting a losing battle against Greta's teenage outbursts in social media. After Greta was named Person of Year by Time Magazine in December 2019, U.S. President Donald Trump tweeted, ""Greta must work on her Anger Management problem, then go to a good old-fashioned movie with a friend! Chill Greta, Chill!" What Trump's generation can't grasp is that Greta represents an inestimably large undercurrent that is inevitably nudging the world toward more sustainable practices by thrusting an environmentalist vision into the forefront of everyone's minds. What she preaches today will inevitably happen tomorrow. If you don't listen up, you could lose a lot of money by investing in oil and gas companies that inevitably will be no more lucrative than a laundromat.

When I watch this predictable turn of events playing out in social media, I feel the same sense of trepidation that I felt in my gut at the beginning of the Lloyd's of London scandal in 1991, when investors who had blindly joined London's insurance market were bankrupted by billions of dollars in asbestos claims. It's the same feeling of foreboding that came over me in the months leading to the subprime mortgage collapse in 2007, when investors lost everything on bonds backed by mortgages for which homeowners had lied about their income on application forms. The last time I felt this way was in northern Italy, Europe's vortex in the COVID-19 pandemic, during my skiing trip with my family in February 2020.

As I've already explained, each of these crises spiraled out of control for the same reasons. First, the leaders in whom we had placed our confidence, from heads of state to chief executive officers, were so far behind the curve that they never saw it coming. Second, the vast majority of investors panicked en masse, driving each other over the cliff like lemmings. In the end, the people who got hurt the most were the least informed – and the last to pull the plug.

There is absolutely no doubt in my mind that anyone who has invested their hard-earned money in companies that engage in controversial practices will end up like the victims of the Lloyd's scandal, the subprime mortgage collapse, or stock market crash of February 2020. It's going to be the same old story all over again.

At this point if you require further evidence of change in the air, look no farther than the Environmental, Social, and Governance (ESG) criteria that a growing number of fund managers are using to screen potential investments. If this abbreviation sounds boring, then be bored at your peril. ESG is a new scorecard that fund managers use to help them navigate through any unsuspected landmines.

The most immediate losers of this high-stakes game will be companies that chalk up the lowest environmental scores, including the mining and oil and gas industries that have fallen into Greta's crosshairs, like Royal Dutch Shell and ExxonMobil. There also bottling companies, like Coca-Cola Co., Nestle and PepsiCo., which have been labeled as the world's three largest plastic polluters for two years in a row. The manufacturing of plastic, and its disposal, contributes to climate change by generating astronomically high levels of greenhouse gas. For a close-up view of the environmental impact on our oceans, just take a walk along the nearest beach.

Businesses with low social scores are often in the tobacco, gambling, alcohol, firearms industries, or are involved in military weapons development. You should avoid these companies as if you were marching around a minefield.

Low governance scores can be a function of a whole host of issues, starting with how ethnically diverse the board of directors is. When you leaf through a company's annual report, just take a look at the photographs of the directors. Ask yourself, how many of them are women?

On the flip side, ESG scores allow you to build a list of companies to invest in – that is, the companies with high scores. The environmental criteria consider how a company performs as a steward of nature, including frighteningly detailed calculations of how much waste and pollution it causes. The social criteria examine how well a company manages relationships with employees, suppliers, customers and the communities where it operates, for example, by donating a percentage of profits to communities in need. Governance criteria deal with corporate leadership, executive pay, audits, internal controls and shareholder rights -- for example, accuracy and transparency in accounting.

It hardly comes as a surprise that the most ESG-compliant businesses around the world are in technology, health care and consumer staples. Not by coincidence, these businesses have a miniscule carbon footprint compared with airlines and oil and gas companies. I monitor them closely to see what investments they are making that could ultimately raise their ESG scores even higher. One such company, Burberry, the London-listed fashion retailer, claims to be mitigating its environmental impact by "storing carbon at source and removing it from the atmosphere," which involves developing a fully traceable organic cotton supply.

In fact, the top five ESG-compliant businesses in the U.S. read like a Who's Who of the hottest growth stocks listed on NASDAQ since the late 1990s -- Microsoft, Apple, Amazon, Facebook and Google. All of them are already using renewable energy, taking a significant burden off the global electrical grid.

The irony is that no matter how small the carbon footprint of each of these companies is, the internet still uses more than 10 percent of the world's electricity supply. Most of the energy consumed by data centers is used for air conditioning used to keep the servers cool.

Building these centers, too, carries an environmental cost, which these technology heavyweights are investing heavily to mitigate. Amazon is investing $2 billion in "sustainable and decarbonizing" technologies in an effort to eliminate its carbon footprint. In June 2020, Amazon announced a more aggressive schedule to power its operations with its renewable energy sources, moving the deadline forward by five years to 2025. Microsoft in January 2020 announced its own $1 billion climate fund, which will invest in technology to remove or reduce carbon from the earth's atmosphere. Greta will be pleased.

I believe one reason tech companies are ahead of the game is that it's always been in their DNA to leverage data to their advantage. For any company, ESG is all about using information technology to gather internal company data to prove that it is compliant. It's never been enough to simply measure carbon emissions. The companies that achieve higher ESG scores are constantly running algorithms and creating models to develop better ways to improve their compliance. Going forward, advancements in IT can only help businesses prove to governments, consumers and investors just how ESG-compliant they really are by displaying progressively minute levels of detailed data. Businesses that can't leverage data will fall behind.

Companies that invest heavily in ESG compliance will only attract more capital. Companies that fall behind will find that their costs of raising capital will increase. CEOs see it as a way to make money when it's done right -- and a way to lose significant amounts when it's done wrong. For any investor, this is a multi-trillion-dollar tailwind that you can get behind by closely examining how thorough a company's ESG compliance really is. Bank of America Merrill Lynch recently predicted that up to $20 trillion could be invested in institutional funds that manage ESG stock over the next three decades.

In its passive form, this game is also well underway at the retail level. Many asset managers offer exchange-traded funds (ETFs) that claim to track the most ESG-compliant companies. The iShares ESG MSCI USA ETF has nearly $7 billion in assets, 27 percent of which are in information technology, followed by 13 percent in health care and only 12 percent in industrials.

You don't have to rely on published ESG scores to find out how socially responsible a company is. The providers of these scores, such as Thomas Reuters, Bloomberg and MSCI, charge thousands of dollars a year for this information. Anyone can glean enough information to make an investment decision from a company's annual report. Although it may look boring, it's actually worth reading. Every company designs and structures its annual report differently, giving you a sense of its attitude toward corporate governance. One company's annual report can look like a box-ticking exercise while another annual report can look like it's been written with enthusiasm.

Many companies are sprucing up their image to appeal to the growing number of investors who care about their communities and want to save the planet. More than ever before, companies are emblazoning their websites with eco-friendly images as a PR strategy. It's not unusual for oil and gas companies to post photographs of renewable energy sources and trees on the covers of their annual reports. Royal Dutch Shell published a picture of a forest in its 2019 annual report while photographs in Duke Energy's annual report depicted solar panels.

Of course, any company can use window dressing to make itself look far more ESG-compliant than it really is. In the oil and gas industry, in particular, don't let photographs alone convince you that the business is becoming environmentally friendly. Instead, take the trouble to look at how much of the electricity that the company uses comes from renewables. For example, while BP publicizes its renewable business, the lion's share (90 percent) of its capital investment goes into oil and gas and only 3 percent into renewable sources.

Compared with Coca-Cola and Pepsi's investor relations websites, Nestle's stands out. Nestle goes into far more detail than its competitors about its strategy to become a more sustainable company. Nestle's stated goal is to make 100 percent of its packaging recyclable or reusable by 2025. The company used a total of 1.5 million metric tons of plastic in 2019. However, during that year, the company managed to avoid using another 142,000 metric tons of plastic, which would have been enough to build 14 Eiffel Towers out of plastic. By 2030, Nestle wants to collect as many plastic bottles as it produces. They also want to raise awareness about recycling and encourage governments to promote it.

Not surprisingly, Nestle is a leading ESG-compliant business in Europe. Others include Roche Holding and AstraZeneca in health care, and ASML Holding and SAP SE in information technology.

Businesses that talk the talk – but can't walk the walk -- could find themselves being quickly rated downward on the ESG scale. Unlike Nestle, Pepsi and Cola-Cola have not publicly committed to reducing their plastic footprint by 2025 or even to investing in reusable or recyclable plastic bottles. The farthest Coca-Cola has gone is to promise to collect one bottle or can for each one sold by 2030, and to manufacture every plastic Coke bottle using at least 50 percent recycled plastic by 2030.

Pepsi's stated goal is to make 100 percent of its packaging recyclable, compostable or biodegradable by 2025.

It's not just their reputations that are stake. In addition to being tarnished with low ESG scores, these companies could find themselves parting with cold, hard cash. In February 2020, the European Commission, which is the executive body of the European Union, met to discuss a proposed tax of 80 euro cents (or 87 U.S. cents) per kilogram of non-recycled plastic. If passed, the tax could be applied to at least 7.5 million tons of plastic waste that never gets recycled every year in the 27 nations of the EU.

The proposed carbon tax is a last-ditch effort by the EU to fill two yawning gaps in its seven-year budget, which was proposed at a whopping 1.13 trillion euros ($1.23 trillion). First, the EU lost 10 billion euros in value-added tax from the UK after Brexit. Second, most businesses slowed down to such a severe extent during the COVID-19 pandemic that Europe's 27 national governments are facing severe shortfalls in the collection of corporate taxes.

In the U.S., environmental lawyers are urging state governments to impose carbon taxes not only to make up for tax revenue that was lost during the pandemic, but also to keep the air as clean as it has become since factories, cars, trucks, airplanes and construction equipment stopped belching soot at maximum capacity in late February 2020. During the pandemic, carbon emissions fell by an average of five percent globally. In New York City, which enjoyed an even more precipitous relief from fossil fuel emissions across the board, environmental lawyers are urging lawmakers to "lock in" such emissions reductions permanently with a carbon tax.

Companies that can't play this game should take their marbles home. Those that wind up with low ESG scores will attract less capital, which could result in their stock being downgraded from "buy" to "sell" by analysts on Wall Street over time. Mining companies, for example, have low ESG scores due to their high level of emissions and high numbers of deaths of workers on the job, leading lenders and investors to starve the industry of badly needed capital. Ultimately, some privately held companies will be reluctant to go public if they're afraid of what their ESG score will look like. They will see no profit in raising a public profile if they're seen to be non-compliant.

Rio Tinto, one of the largest iron ore producers in the world, was recently in the firing line after the wanton destruction of a 46,000-year-old aboriginal site to extend its mining operation. These religious sites are not only greatly revered by the aboriginals but highly valued by historians, scholars and archeologists. It's tragic that a part of history was lost forever in the pursuit of profit. Greta, please don't look now.

Wells Fargo of San Francisco allegedly engaged in fraud by opening millions of new accounts for existing customers without their permission. In a practice known as cross-selling, or offering different services to those which the customers had originally applied for, Wells collected fees on the new accounts without even notifying the clients. This has been very damaging for its reputation and share price.

Wells Fargo has been continually dogged by poor headlines around corporate governance. Over the last five years, the bank's share price has fallen more than 50 percent. On the other hand, JP Morgan's share price has risen 50 percent during the same period. The lesson is that if a company is deemed to have poor governance, then run for the hills.

Just a dozen years ago, socially responsible investing (SRI) was left for dead in the wake of the financial crisis. Portfolios that managers had filled with stocks that only met socially responsible criteria took ages to recover from the financial crisis of 2008, and some SRI managers went out of business.

In its current form, however, ethical investing is emerging with a vengeance as a clear bull trend that anyone can make money from. Now that I am running my own family office, one of the first steps I take before buying a company's stock is to think about how ESG-compliant it is. If the company's ESG score is not high, I won't bother with any further research on it.

I just won't buy its shares. More importantly, if you think Greta would give the company the thumbs up, it's certainly worth doing more research.

CHAPTER NINETEEN: THE PETROLEUM LAUNDROMAT

Like Greta Thunberg's disability, mine has never prevented me from cutting through the absolute B.S. spouted by multinationals that present themselves as rulers of the global economy. Ever since I bought my first stock at the age of 12, I could see clearly that oil and gas companies – and the companies that operate the pipelines that carry oil and gas to refineries -- had no brighter a future than my father's laundromat ever did.

In the 1980s, everyone argued that oil and gas was a sunset industry because the multinationals were rapidly depleting the earth's known oil and gas reserves. But I've always known the truth. This is an industry that has been slammed by technological disruption. Just as retail shopping was disrupted by the internet, the oil and gas industry has been disrupted by cleaner, cheaper, renewable energy -- mainly solar and wind-powered. The cost of renewable energy has fallen to a point where it is knocking out older forms of energy generation. In addition, environmental protection regulations have raised the cost of producing oil and gas.

More recently, as I've already explained, the Greta Principle threatens to put petroleum explorers and producers out of business altogether. You can thank social media for the phenomenal growth of Greta's influence over consumers and corporations alike. Second, you can thank the rise of Environmental, Social and Governance (ESG) criteria in investing.

Of course, CEOs and other senior managers of oil and gas companies certainly know where they need to go. Yet, given the sweeping change that would be required to bring their antiquated business models and deeply entrenched practices even close to something sustainable, the cost to shareholders would be intolerably high.

At best, no fossil-fuel-based energy company will ever be anything more than a value trap for investors. Integrated oil and gas companies no smaller than Total of France are currently trading at a discount to book value, meaning that you can buy stock in these companies for even less than all of their equipment and property are worth. This must be disconcerting for CEOs because it's like having built a house for $100,000 with a plan to sell it for $1 million – only to sell it for $80,000. If the companies were to go bankrupt tomorrow, according to the logic of a value investor, you would turn a profit after the assets were sold at auction.

As the oil and gas industry contracts, clever operators will undoubtedly lower their production costs, making companies more profitable and thus more attractive to investors. My prediction is that the last players left standing will be those with the lowest production costs.

Keep your eye on the exit. Having had their valuations beaten down, oil and gas stocks can expect to enjoy some very aggressive stock rallies. If anything, I would use such a rally as an opportunity to exit.

As I've already explained, just because a company is a bargain does not mean it's worth buying. As we all know, when a store decides to sell merchandise at a discount, consumers find it very enticing. But I view these discounted items as products that were just priced too high in the first place. If stocks languish on the bargain basement racks, do your best not to be drawn in by the enticing fluorescent yellow-and-red "Sale" and "50% off" signs. When stocks are priced at a bargain, I view the seller just wanting to get them off his books, and I'm therefore never in a rush to invest.

Thanks to the value-oriented mandates of pension funds, companies like Royal Dutch Shell and ExxonMobil are highly likely to be held by your parents' pension plans. On average, they still account for five percent of the holdings of all passive index funds. The psychology behind this fact of life evokes old

TV episodes of Dallas where Sue Ellen Ewing, played by Linda Grey, wore these great big shoulder pads. Value investors seem to be holding onto oil and gas stocks in the hope that they will come back into fashion someday. Like the shoulder pads, these stocks will stay out of fashion perpetually. If I were a pension fund manager, I would dump these stocks even if their prices were cut in half overnight.

Oil and gas companies are like Eastman Kodak, which once ruled the world with a product that was disrupted by technology. Kodak revolutionized photography by producing point-and-click cameras that were easy for anyone to use, making film development and printing processes cheap enough for anyone to afford, and introducing the concept of the snapshot to the global consumer culture. Kodak could never be accused of ignoring the digital photography revolution. In fact, the company invented and patented the world's first digital camera in 1975. What finally drove Kodak into bankruptcy was a rapid decline in demand for the film that had always been the company's mainstay. Kodak fell too far behind its Japanese competitors in the development of its digital camera business to recover its footing.

Moreover, the petroleum industry is plagued by fluctuations in global oil prices. The problem is three-fold. First of all, according to the Energy Information Administration, the U.S. was sitting on vast proved reserves of 43.8 billion barrels of oil and 504.5 trillion cubic trillion feet of natural gas at the end of 2018. During that year, petroleum companies discovered new, proved reserves of 4.7 billion barrels of oil and 40.2 trillion cubic feet of natural gas.

All told, the U.S. is now the largest oil and gas producer in the world with about 18 percent of total production, followed by Saudi Arabia at 12 percent. Oil production in the U.S. has increased from around 5.1 million barrels a day in December 2008 to more than 12.8 million as of February 2020. With total global demand for oil estimated at 100 million barrels a day, the U.S. is displacing OPEC as the world's oil broker.

Secondly, technological developments in hydraulic fracking have allowed the U.S. to tap into huge oil and gas resources that were previously uneconomic to access. In addition to the new proved reserves that came online in 2018, the U.S., Geological Survey reported that an unproved 46 billion barrels of oil, 280 trillion cubic feet of natural gas, and 20 billion barrels of natural gas liquids had been discovered in shale formations under the Permian Basin of West Texas in November of that year. The Permian find more than doubled the country's estimated oil reserves, and it increased natural gas reserves by 55 percent.

Ultimately, the supply of oil has grown so large – along with the amount of capital at risk – that it is in nobody's interest to cut production. While the oil and gas industry makes up only eight percent of U.S. gross domestic product, it represents 30 percent of Russia's GDP and a breathtaking 86 percent of Saudi Arabia's GDP. So, it's Russia and Saudi Arabia that suffer the most when they cut production. By the time oil prices had fallen by 79 percent, from $61.72 on December 27, 2019, to just $12.78 on April 27, 2020, multinational oil executives and OPEC leaders were desperate to get as much oil as possible out of the ground immediately, in order to counter-act the falls in price.

Third, global climate change has made consumers reluctant to burn oil and gas, so our governments are urging us not to. Thanks largely to the Greta Principle, people are more conscious about their carbon footprint today than ever before. New car buyers are far more likely to buy an electric vehicle (EV) than they were a few years ago. In February 2020, Shell surveyed more than 1,000 people in the UK, where the government plans to ban the sales of gasoline, diesel and hybrid gas-electric cars by 2035. The survey found that 70 percent of them were considering purchasing an EV as their next car. Findings like that are enough to make the petroleum industry – and oil prices – look like toast.

Oil prices are unlikely to return to the peak they reached in 2013, when they hovered around $108 a barrel. One catalyst was China emerging in rude health from the global financial crisis of 2008, when oil had traded at just $63 a barrel, which drove a dramatic increase in domestic oil consumption. Another catalyst was the Deepwater Horizon oil spill in the Gulf of Mexico in April 2010, when Brent crude was trading at $85 a barrel. In the manner that the Dieselgate scandal resulted in Volkswagen's headquarters being raided by police and led to tighter regulatory scrutiny over vehicle emissions tests by automakers, BP fell into the crosshairs of federal prosecutors investigating the cause of an environmental disaster. In the end, higher insurance premiums, mandatory third-party inspections, tighter regulatory scrutiny, and costly delays in production combined to push oil prices higher over the next three years.

Since then, oil prices have crept up to a few less impressive peaks before sliding back down again. More recently, in December 2019, the initial public offering of Aramco, Saudi Arabia's national oil company, valued the business at $1.7 trillion. An offer to buy equity in a state enterprise that Saudi princes have milked for half a century should be enough to make any investor want to run for the hills. The princes could tell that oil revenue would drop in the future, the burden of which they would rather share with their shareholders. However, investors were blindly attracted to Aramco's generous dividend yield of four percent, and the stock price performed relatively well. These factors contributed to an increase in global oil prices, to $63.27 on January 6, 2020, from $52.45 on October 3, 2019. In response, the governments of Saudi Arabia and Russia both announced that they would raise production to compete for market share. The result was that crude prices fell by one-third. Finally, Aramco's share price dropped, by ten percent, on March 9, 2020.

Let's put another company, like Royal Dutch Shell, under the microscope for a moment. If you are tempted to buy the company's stock after it fell by 65 percent, to $60.96 on January 6 to $21.62 on March 18, 2020, thanks to the COVID-19 pandemic, think again. Would you confess to Greta Thunberg that you had bought the shares? If not, don't buy them.

Another reason you would not want to admit to having invested in Shell – or any multinational in the oil and gas industry, for that matter – is that the business you buy today inevitably will look entirely different in the near future. Under the leadership of its respected CEO, Ben van Beurden, Shell became the world's second-largest publicly listed energy company when it bought BG Group for $70 billion in 2015.

However, the BG acquisition showed such a blatant lack of foresight that the management team might as well have been wearing horse blinders when it signed off on the deal. Valuing BG at 50 percent more than its share price at the time, the deal transformed Shell's conservative net debt into a net debt equivalent to more than half of its current market capitalization. After oil prices fell, dragging down net income by 46 percent in the first quarter of 2020, Shell cut dividends for the first time since the Second World War, and it suspended the next tranche of a program to buy back its own stock from investors. To make matters worse, shareholders will be paying to prop up Shell's underfunded pension plan, which will be $7.3 billion in the red, for decades to come.

None of this would have mattered to Greta had Shell not become an even bigger polluter through the deal -- over which she would certainly throw one of her characteristically obsessive tantrums. Because BG owned prized liquefied natural gas (LNG) assets, the acquisition dramatically increased the amount of pollution that Shell produces. What is remarkable about the LNG business is that it allows countries like Australia and America to liquify their highly pollutive gas and ship it to other continents. The gas is frozen and loaded aboard tankers that each carry a row of high-pressure spherical tanks containing 4.4 million cubic feet of LNG -- enough to heat 300,000 homes for a year and even fuel the stoves in their kitchens. These pot-bellied tankers also burn a lot of fuel on the journey between continents. Power plants in China and Japan, where domestic gas prices are higher than in Australia or the U.S., eagerly sign 30-

year contracts at what they consider generous discounts. They thaw out this cheap heating fuel and burn it to generate electricity. Shareholders have raised no objection to the company's fast-growing LNG business despite its obvious contradiction to Shell's stated goal to become "carbon neutral" by 2050.

When an LNG tanker drops anchor at the port where its precious cargo will be degasified, the gas flows literally across continents through steel pipelines that, at first glance, might look like a safe investment for a do-it-yourself stock-picker. More pipelines run through the U.S. than anywhere else in the world, carrying gas through various networks of pipelines for a total 1.3 million miles. According to the Interstate Natural Gas Association of America, North America will need to spend $23 billion annually through 2035 on new gas infrastructure to support expected growth in consumption and demand, which will be led by new LNG and petrochemical plants in Louisiana and Texas.

Some of the largest operators of these pipelines actually trade on the stock market, where investors have always valued them as highly as telecommunications companies. But investors who buy into these pipeline companies eventually find out the hard way what their real value is.

The problem with these pipeline companies is that the argument to invest in them has always been monopolistic. The pipelines were seen as toll roads that LNG producers could supposedly never bypass – and that the pipeline companies could always afford to keep expanding to new ports where LNG was being offloaded at new degasification plants, or new "tight" gas reserves where fracking technology was being deployed. Some investors even made the mistake of comparing the pipeline networks with old-fashioned telephone exchanges – until they were effectively bypassed by cellular telephone technology.

The poster child for this fallacy is Kinder Morgan, which carries 40 percent of all natural gas consumed in the U.S. through its pipelines. Until 2015, Kinder Morgan attracted investors with generous dividends and fantastic promises that its pipeline network, which connects with every major supply basin, could only grow with constant discoveries of new natural gas deposits and ever-increasing demand in urban areas. Kinder Morgan shares traded at such astronomical prices that its stock certificates might as well have been printed on gold leaf until investors finally figured out that the company had fallen so deeply into debt from expanding its pipeline network to keep up with growing demand for LNG, that it would have to slash its generous dividends. So Kinder Morgan's share price plummeted by 68 percent during seven fraught months in 2015, to $15.14 on December 18 from $44.57 on April 23, and it has not risen above $23.13 since then. As of May 2020, Kinder Morgan has a current market capitalization of $35 billion, equal to debt of also $35 billion.

If only the whole oil and gas industry would just come out and say, "Well, folks, it's been a gas, but we are finally going out of business." Then the world would be a cleaner place to live with more breathable air and clearer skies -- as we saw at the beginning of the COVID-19 epidemic when airports shut down, commercial airlines stopped flying, there were far fewer cars and trucks on the highways, and many factories stopped belching soot out of their smokestacks. The world would also be a safer place for investors who have started to realize that the future is in companies that are based on digital technology which was monetized over the internet more than a century after Nikolaus August Otto patented the four-stroke engine in 1876. A case in point: In May 2020, ExxonMobil's market capitalization was valued at slightly less than that of Netflix – and ExxonMobil's share price had done nothing to please investors since the turn of the Twenty-First Century. Because energy makes up only five percent of the S&P 500, you can still expect to beat the indexes even if you never own stock in a single petroleum company. So why bother?

CHAPTER TWENTY: DON'T GET TOO EXCITED ABOUT RENEWABLES!

As the oil and gas industry becomes progressively disrupted by renewable energy technology, investors are, quite logically, getting increasingly excited about companies that claim to be producing clean energy. They find solar energy particularly sexy, sometimes even comparing solar panel manufacturers with makers of the latest flat screen TVs.

Not every fairy tale has a happy ending, unfortunately. The simple truth is that renewable energy is no safer a bastion of capitalism than Big Oil was ever a good steward of the environment.

Thanks to intense competition for China's vast, largely untapped renewable energy market, manufacturers of everything from solar panels to windmill blades are operating on razor-thin margins that make them no more lucrative than Korean consumer electronics manufacturers. While renewable energy may sound as enticing as consumer electronics, investors in both industries are getting burned.

A very good rule of thumb is to only invest in businesses that have operating margins above ten percent. If there are any issues in the supply chain -- or a general slowdown of the economy, which we saw during the COVID-19 pandemic – companies with higher margins will be less likely to come cap-in-hand to shareholders. The fear is that companies with low margins might issue new stock to pay their bills, which would dilute existing shareholders.

The only companies involved in renewable energy that have higher profit margins – and are thus worth investing in -- are utilities that generate electricity. The most attractive ones are in the process of becoming less dependent on nuclear energy, coal, oil or gas--fired power plants. They are moving toward cheaper sources of energy, mainly solar and wind, the costs of which have fallen since 2019. This will improve their ability to produce cheaper electricity, ultimately making consumers the real winners of the renewable energy game.

European suppliers of renewable energy seem to be ahead of the curve. Perhaps the most powerful driver of the shift to renewable energy on the continent is Germany, which has been called the "the world's first major renewable energy economy." Approximately 52 percent of Germany's electricity came from renewables during the first quarter of 2020. Paving the way for the rest of Europe, the German government has declared that all nuclear and coal-fired power stations will be decommissioned by 2030.

The most profitable publicly listed electrical utilities that generate a majority of their capacity from renewable sources are all in Europe. Iberdrola of Spain, for example, had a healthy 16.2 percent operating profit margin at the end of March 2020. During the five years through 2022, the company plans to have invested $13 billion in renewables. The company has set a target to produce "practically zero" emissions in Europe by 2030, and to become carbon neutral by 2050 globally.

Electric utilities that can drive down their cost of electricity generation by investing in renewables will win this game. For example, Enel of Italy, which had an operating profit margin of 17.3 percent at the end of March, is also investing significantly in renewables, which now make up 50 percent of the company's total electricity generation. The company is evidently on track to reach its 2050 target to have 80 percent of its electricity come from renewables. Enel, despite its dramatic progress in installing new renewable capacity, still generates 15 percent of its electricity from nuclear power plants. Those that still depend on nuclear energy will never be any more profitable than laundromats. Not only is nuclear power one of the most expensive sources of electricity, but it also comes with extreme environmental burdens. The Fukushima Daichi nuclear plant in northern Japan cost $187 billion to decommission and clean up after its meltdown in March 2011. Contamination caused by a fire at a nuclear reactor in Sellafield, England, in 1957 ultimately cost British taxpayers £70 billion ($85.5 billion) to clean up.

If you include the inevitable costs of decommissioning a nuclear power station and the huge expense of long-term nuclear waste storage, then nuclear power is much more expensive than any other energy source in the long run. No matter how clean the renewable technology that electric utilities are installing happens to be, the fact that they are still exposed to the risk of a nuclear accident means that your investment in these companies could be toast overnight.

The country that appears to be the farthest behind the curve is the United States, where the government might as well have been asleep at the wheel for the last half-century. President Donald Trump has demonstrated in numerous public speeches that he doesn't understand wind power, calling the "ugly" wind turbines "bird killers" and "monsters".

But change could be afoot. Recently, the Democratic presidential runner, Joe Biden, proposed a $2 trillion plan to escalate the use of clean energy in power generation, transportation and buildings. If elected, this would imply a major acceleration in clean infrastructure spending. Drawing a parallel with Europe, Goldman Sachs estimate that a global shift to net zero policies would accelerate annual capital expenditure in renewables and networks by more than 150 percent.

According to the U.S. Energy Information Administration, 63 percent of the country's electricity generation comes from fossil fuels, including 38 percent natural gas and 23 percent coal. The power plants that produce all of this electricity will become worthless as newer cleaner, cheaper alternative energy technology sweeps across the U.S. in the decades to come. Currently, renewable energy makes up only 17.5 percent of capacity, including 1.8 percent solar, 7.3 percent wind, and the remainder in hydropower.

Duke Energy, one of the country's largest electric utilities, states on its website that the company is proudly attempting to prolong the lifetime of its nuclear reactors. From my point of view, this Charlotte, North Carolina, company is just increasing its liability for a potential nuclear accident and delaying the inevitable decommissioning cost. Only two percent of Duke's net output came from hydropower and solar facilities in 2019. An astonishing 26 percent came from natural gas, 35 percent from nuclear power, and 27 percent from coal-fired power plants.

For the time being, the real beneficiaries of renewable energy are consumers who will enjoy lower electric bills -- and the environment, which will suffer less pollution. Unfortunately, investors will not always reap a financial return from a clean conscience. Investors started getting excited about solar energy in 2008, when they bid up First Solar stock, one of the largest manufacturers of solar modules, to the point that its market capitalization reached nearly $20 billion. Since then, the stock price has plummeted by 85 percent. The stock now at the same level where it started trading in 2007.

While the solar energy market has certainly grown at exponential rates, this growth has come at the cost of profit margins. First Solar recorded an operating loss of $83 million in 2019. In 2020, the company is expected to post an operating income of $258 million on turnover of $2.6 billion, which will leave the company with a negligible profit margin of around 1 percent.

The problem with any manufacturer of electrical equipment is that this is a low-margin business. First Solar bears comparison with LG Electronics, the South Korean manufacturer of flat-screen TVs. LG's stock price has flatlined for nearly 20 years. While LG's TV business enjoys has a handsome market share of 18.7 percent worldwide, the business overall has had a miserable profit margin between three percent and 4.4 percent over the last five years. In other words, every TV that LG sells with a $1,000 price tag will only make a $40 profit for the company.

Like First Solar, LG's business model exists to dominate the global market with huge volumes and low prices. This model leaves no fat on the bone. The real beneficiary is the consumer – not the shareholder. The risk of such low margins is that the slightest hiccup in the supply chain or a slowdown in the economy -- both of which we witnessed during the COVID-19 pandemic -- can lead to massive losses.

In the renewable energy industry, manufacturers of wind turbines and other equipment used in wind farms have enjoyed fatter margins than their counterparts in the solar energy business. There is absolutely no doubt that there will be greater demand for wind turbines as the growth of the world's electricity grid accelerates. However, it is not certain that wind manufacturers can increase their margins in the future.

Even Vestas Wind Systems of Denmark, the biggest wind turbine manufacturer in the world, operates in an extremely competitive environment. The company faces stiff competition from Siemens Gamesa Renewable, GE and other behemoths. Vestas nearly doubled its sales in the last five years, during which the company has reported volatile margins between 8 percent and 13.8 percent. The margins have been as unpredictable as the direction that the wind blows.

Before I will even consider renewable energy companies an attractive investment, there will have to be a concerted effort by leaders of the industry to make it more profitable – whether or not they are trying to save the planet. A clean conscience will never be enough of an incentive for investors in any industry – not even renewable energy -- although Greta may bathe in the solar glow and would be happy with investments in renewable energy. Normal people like you and I will have to be convinced that they will reap the benefits of the stock market before we will be willing to sink our hard-earned money into renewable energy assets.

CHAPTER TWENTY-ONE: THE MAGIC CARPET PRINCIPLE

Whenever my family and I take a vacation, our flight is often delayed. Adding to the stress of being in an airport, Georgie and I have to call the taxi company that was supposed to pick us up at the other end and tell them that we're running an hour late. Or, if our flight is canceled, we have to cancel not only the taxi ride but also our hotel reservation. What annoys me the most is that when we finally do arrive at our hotel, the front desk clerks always act surprised, looking for our reservations as though they hadn't expected our arrival.

It's the misery and stress of travel that has led me to imagine how the travel industry could work out the bugs in a manner that investors such as I would find attractive. Imagine what a difference it would make if, for instance, clever AI technology enabled an airline like EasyJet to inform all the online platforms that had booked the rest of your vacation – those of the taxi company, your hotel, and even the restaurants and opera houses where you had made reservations – that your flight was delayed or canceled. The companies that resolve the issues around the last mile traveled are investments that have clear tailwinds.

I envisage an all-encompassing, door-to-door, cloud-based platform where the local taxi you have booked to take you from your home to the airport informs you of a road accident and arrives ahead of schedule. Then EasyJet automatically informs Uber that your flight is delayed, Uber automatically informs your hotel that you will arrive after your requested check-in time, and the Uber that drops you off informs the hotel of your expected time of arrival so that the front desk staff can get your room keys ready and even prepare your check-in documents before your arrival. The technology would give each mode of transportation live updates on your travel information, making travel ever more seamless.

I mean, really, just think about it. As we can infer from my earlier discussion of Amazon and Google, advancements in AI and location-based technology have already reached the point where all the glitches can be removed from the last mile traveled. In the very near future, you should be able to type your current location and holiday destination into a website and leave it up to AI to give you the price options for your entire trip across different platforms. Websites like Booking.com, to which I had entrusted my family's skiing vacation at the beginning of the COVID-19 pandemic in Northern Italy, would find the cheapest options among decent hotels, allow you to pay for the whole holiday and all transportation involved via Paypal, and relieve your stress from the moment you leave your doorstep. This would include the taxi from your home to the airport, the flight, your taxi from the airport to your hotel, and even your hotel, too. A few key players, such as Uber, PayPal, and Google Maps could lay down the train tracks with Booking.com for such an interconnected style of travel.

Although sites like Booking.com already allow you to book all these travel necessities on a single platform, what they still don't do is talk to each other in real time. As an investor, the only way I can think of to monetize the future of travel is to own big digital platforms that have the ability to create such a marriage between travel platforms. The companies that can develop the technology capable of resolving the issue with the last mile traveled will be the only investment I'll ever make in travel. The future of travel is being able to book the whole trip from door to door using one platform that will be linked to other platforms such as Uber and EasyJet, enabling each platform to communicate and create end-to-end seamless travel. This is indeed the new package holiday for the modern era.

Like most industries, the travel business is being disrupted by technology, so my instinct is to gravitate toward it. The problem is that it's all over the place. There is no clear leader – and the killer app doesn't even exist yet. As a result, any investment in the travel sector has its risks.

An investment where you're most likely to lose money is a hotel chain. Not only do travelers have more accommodation to choose from on the internet, thanks to Airbnb, but they can even compare rates for hotel rooms with those for private accommodation, thanks to Booking.com.

The hospitality business is being most severely disrupted by Airbnb, which is private and thus can't be owned by me, you or any other investor on the stock market. Named after an air mattress that Brian Chesky, the company's founder, and his roommates rented out on their living room floor, AirBNB now has 4 million spaces for rent around the world in 65,500 cities in 191 countries. Thus far, the company has had 400 million customers, roughly 60 percent of whom are Millennials. The message: AirBNB is the way of the future.

The one publicly traded company that is worth owning in the travel industry is Booking Holdings. That's why I use its website, Booking.com, to find a comfortable bed whenever I can – just to reassure myself that their service still meets my expectations. Recently, one of my daughters, Jemima, went on a sporting trip to Oxford, and the rest of us went along to watch for a few days. Instead of a booking a hotel, Georgie booked a two-bedroom apartment on Booking.com. It was cheaper than a hotel, with more space than a typical hotel room. Instead of room service, we ordered Uber Eats from the restaurant around the corner. I left that apartment confident that I had bought the right stock.

Booking.com is emblematic of the transformation that the internet has brought to the once arduous process of booking vacations. Gone are the days of flipping through glossy travel brochures and standing in line at a travel agency. Booking a vacation now is as seamless and stress-free as buying a pair of socks on Amazon. While the internet allows people to reserve a hotel room, round-trip flights, excursions and even rental cars with just a few mouse clicks, Booking.com allows them to do all this on a single platform. Their website offers hotel reviews, easy payment methods and even lets you cancel three days before your trip – or sometimes even on the same day. That's why many customers book three hotels at a time before doing their homework – and then cancel the two they don't like.

Booking.com is a more complicated company than meets the eye. It also owns Open Table, an online restaurant reservation platform, and KAYAK, a website that searches and compares prices for travel itineraries including rental cars, airline tickets and accommodation. Its legacy accommodation service covers 460,000 hotels and 2.21 million homes in more than 230 countries.

This asset-light business generates massive cash returns for shareholders. Enjoying a luxurious operating margin of 30.2 percent, Booking Holdings only has two major costs. One is in the clever IT engineers who work on developing their slick and easy-to-navigate online platforms. The other is cleverly targeted online advertising through Google and Facebook.

The company doesn't seem to be worried about its future. Over the last five years, Booking Holdings has bought back nearly 20 percent of its own stock.

That's one reason why Booking Holdings was too expensive to own until late February 2020, when its shares fell 40 percent from $1,990 to $1,177 on March 16, 2020, during the pandemic on fears that the hotel industry had been decimated. Of course, this was a perfect entry point for long-term investors like me. There is no question that the hospitality and travel industry will continue to be impacted by COVID-19 over the next few years. Yet as wealth continues to grow over the years, more and more people are going to travel.

No other travel business has profit margins that come close to those of Booking Holdings. Its archrival, Expedia, has operating margin of only 7 percent. The issue is that Expedia owns too many brands in the travel space – nearly 20, including Trivago and Carrentals.com. This makes the company more difficult to analyze. Expedia is run by the great entrepreneur Barry Diller, who has built the company through numerous acquisitions. Unlike Booking Holdings, Expedia has piled up debt over the last five years.

In the taxi business, the closest comparison with Booking Holdings is Uber. Unlike Booking Holdings, though, Uber is a loss-making company, and it's forecast to keep making losses for the next three years. Currently valued at $65 billion, Uber certainly has the potential to be a much bigger platform as it becomes more broadly integrated with the entire travel experience. Uber has become so widely accepted by teenagers and adults alike that I believe it has the potential to join PayPal, Google Maps and Booking.com as the railroad tracks for the interconnected future of travel. With this technology, the Uber that takes you to your hotel will inform the hotel of your expected time of arrival, by which time your keys and check-in documents will be waiting for you at the front desk.

Technology is not the only disruptor in the travel industry. The other is budget airlines, which have become so brutally competitive that it's hard to think that a single survivor will be left standing. Even if they stay in business, they'll just never be any more attractive as investments than my father's laundromats were.

Commercial airlines were doomed long before the COVID-19 pandemic forced the world's governments to bail them out. I was in my early twenties when I started to see commercial airlines as a sunset industry. I saw this first-hand when Georgie decided to leave school and become an airline pilot.

When I dropped her off at the Cabair College of Air Training, we discovered to our shock that Georgie was the only woman there. The school didn't even have a women's toilet or shower. She had to share a bathroom with the men.

Civil aviation was still in the Stone Age. It made brokerages in the City of London look very modern by comparison. British Airways pilots were all former Royal Air Force. BA was being drained by its pension obligations, making the airline as fragile as Delta was in June 2020 with its underfunded pension scheme of $5.3 billion. That was equivalent to nearly one-third of Delta's market capitalization.

By the time Georgie had finished flight school, Europe's single market had created an open skies policy. Budget airlines were launching across the Continent. The UK was catching up with the U.S., which had embraced budget airlines since the launch of Southwest Airlines in 1949. Competition became so brutal that the first budget airline Georgie joined, Debonair, went out of business by the time she was qualified to fly the Boeing 737 airliner in 1999.

Cutting a slender figure in her blue pilot's uniform, Georgie walked across the road at Luton airport to an orange hanger where yet another budget airline, EasyJet, was just taking off. The charismatic Greek founder, Stelios Haji-Loannou, who had just ordered a fleet of 737s, eagerly hired Georgie on the spot.

Then came the internet. At one of the company's summer barbeques, while Stelios was flipping burgers on the grill, Georgie and I were sipping cocktails with the sales team. Someone joked about the phone call he kept getting from worried passengers: They wanted to make sure the reservations they had made online had gone through. They didn't trust the internet.

Fast forward two decades, and the internet is the only thing anyone can trust in the travel industry anymore. It the bedrock of Booking Holdings, which is bound to keep growing now that airlines are getting off the ground again. EasyJet resumed flights in June 2020 after a two-and-a-half-month hiatus at only 30 percent capacity with undaunted passengers donning masks. Commercial airlines were getting off the ground thanks to a $25 billion bailout from Washington for the likes of United Airlines, American Airlines and Delta. Lufthansa was offered a 9.9-billion-euro package from the German government. Air France received a 7-billion-euro lifeline.

While COVID-19 will mean fewer passengers in the short term, the long-term growth of commercial airlines is now fully underwritten by governments. Ultimately, airlines will continue to grow as more and more people travel. Governments will reap the tax benefits of tourists spending their money on taxis, bars and restaurants.

If you are looking to make a long-term investment in the travel industry, look away from the graveyard that is the airline industry. Ultimately, the only worthwhile investment will be a seamless online travel app that carries customers from door to door as effortlessly as a magic carpet. Whatever it's called, whoever runs it, the only way the travel industry will ever be of interest to me as an investor is if these apps belong to a publicly listed company.

CHAPTER TWENTY-TWO: IT'S OK TO ADMIT YOU'RE WRONG

Even though I had had no formal schooling beyond St. Edward's College in Liverpool, had never been to business school, and had never studied investing per se, I managed to make money on the stock market at times when market downturns were taking out my competitors.

In addition to looking at the market as sectors and playing themes, what really helped me focus on the market was to see it as a family – a giant, extended family. I would be the last dad in the world to mix my family life with work. Nevertheless, during my 15 years as a portfolio manager, the more I equated the irrational behavior of investors in the stock market with the idiosyncrasies of my own children and relatives, the more I began to see the stock market as a dysfunctional family. I began to draw amazingly illustrative parallels between disclosures by the companies I invested in -- and even announcements by central banks -- with my day-to-day dealings with my family and friends.

To draw a hard line between work and family life, I got into the habit of reserving a taxi in advance on nights out when I knew I would be getting home late so that I wouldn't be too groggy to take care of my children in the morning. This practice came in handy in October 2007 just before the financial crisis when Georgie and I went to a friend's 40th birthday party, which had been planned for months with a band, a DJ, excellent food, and written speeches. Before arriving at the party, I reserved a taxi, using the same reliable yellow cab company we always used, for one o'clock in the morning. We knew we would overstay if we didn't make the reservation. However, I wanted to be sure that the next morning with my four young children would be rewarding -- and not a struggle. My eldest daughter could be counted on to wake me up at 5:30 a.m.

The sacrifice I made was missing the final hours of the party, when it was raging. When I walked in, there were fantastic flower arrangements on each table, an area in the corner of the marquee for a dance floor, and amazing place settings for each guest. By 10:30 p.m., everyone was dancing on the tables. The host would later tell me that the best part started an hour after we left, when the DJ came on and everyone began singing karaoke. The party raged until five o'clock in the morning, half an hour before Annie woke me up.

If only the American consumer had left the party early. In the runup to the highs of the stock market in 2007, Americans were levering themselves up by taking home equity loans and buying things they didn't need. Their party was raging, and U.S. consumption was strong, along with the economy. However, it was all funded by banks that were not going to be paid back.

I noticed the risks in time, and I got off the dance floor early by reducing risk, selling my portfolio, and reaping the reward. I did run the risk of U.S. consumption carrying on, the economy staying strong, and missing the most glorious moments of the party. That month, in October 2007, I took a plane to New York, where I told investors that instead of a play on Chinese infrastructure, my next big theme was going to be shorting Wall Street banks like Lehman Brothers and Merrill Lynch. "The banks are insolvent," I said. Because I'd left the party early, my track record was good, and I was managing $200 million. By June 2008, I was managing more than $1 billion as my theme certainly resonated with some of the top family offices in the U.S..

Just like the time when my family and I were skiing in the Dolomites in February 2020, I had a premonition. It was crystal clear to me that there was far too much leverage in the banking system. UBS, once deemed a conservatively run bank, had a total equity of $38 billion. That was what should have been left of UBS's assets after subtracting all of its liabilities. But UBS had used that $38 billion to extend credit, pushing its total liabilities to around $2 trillion. To put this amount of money in context, at the time $2 trillion was slightly smaller than the British economy. UBS had effectively leveraged its own capital 50 times over, meaning that only a slight decline in asset values in the U.S. housing market, which backed a lot of the bonds that UBS was holding, could wipe out the bank's equity. And it wasn't just UBS. This fiasco smacked of the Lloyd's of London debacle.

In short order, bankers from Wall Street to Zurich were caught out by auditors who had found hundreds of billions of dollars of now worthless subprime bonds on their books. I pondered the bankers' childish behavior in the summer of 2008, when my daughter Jemima would go missing for 15 minutes at a time. We would get suspicious and start looking for her. We would invariably find her hiding under her comforter, under the staircase, or in a closet eating candy. Once we found her sitting in a closet by the front door, eating a huge £1 dairy milk bar. When we politely asked her if she had been eating chocolate, she said "no" and shoved the packet behind her back, but she had chocolate smeared all around her mouth. She reminded me of the bankers who had been binging on subprime bonds that had been backed by mortgages to borrowers who had lied about their incomes on loan applications and could not afford to pay. Until they were caught, they all claimed that they were not exposed to subprime debt. But the reality was that all the bankers had it -- and they didn't even know how much they had.

I managed to keep my cool through the most unnerving of times. I was running the Horseman European Select long-short equity fund. About half of my portfolio was short in 2008, the year the Standard & Poor's 500 fell 37 percent in the most brutal crash since the Great Depression. But the short positions actually drove my fund's returns up that year. The fund posted a 15.73 percent net return in 2008. Just as I would do again in February 2020, I was one of a select few fund managers around the world who had actually found an opportunity in a crisis. I was riding high. What could possibly go wrong?

After central banks around the world printed massive amounts of money, the stock market started to feel as though the lows of March 2009 would never be revisited. In May 2009, after the S&P 500 had rallied 25 percent, I was still running a net short portfolio. The pressure was on. I felt like I was locked in a painful argument with a loved one. When you're convinced you're right, it's always awkward to admit that you might just have been wrong after all. Sometimes you just have to admit you're wrong, suck it up, and move on. Until that month, I had short positions, especially in banks, and they were now costing me money. The stock market was rallying hard, and it was getting painful.

It's more difficult to cut your short positions and go long than the other way around. But I could see the way forward. Even though all my colleagues around me were still very bearish, as the economic data was still very poor, I knew I had to change tack and effectively reverse all my positions. In essence, I was betting on an early recovery for the global economy. As it turned out, I made the right decision. That year, the MSCI Europe Index was actually up 16.18 percent. The whole world was finally on the mend.

You can get yourself locked into a mindset. Being bullish or bearish really is a state of mind. When you're used to being successful, it's hard to change. Despite my success in 2008, there was no guarantee that I would be successful in the years to follow. It was hard for me to tell my investors that I had now turned bullish. The reason they had invested in my fund was that I had been bearish.

However, I was right. Staying short indefinitely would have put me out of business. I have learned that one of the greatest attributes for anybody -- not only in the stock market but in real life -- is to walk away from losing positions and admit when you're wrong.

CHAPTER TWENTY-THREE:
THE TIPPING POINT

When coming out of a deep recession, you can always expect the stock market to be volatile. In November 2010, my children, who were very young at the time, taught me a valuable lesson in how to maintain focus in stressful times. I took them for a ride on the London Eye, the Ferris wheel that towers 441 feet above the South Bank of the River Thames. The sky was gray and thick with clouds. Like an aerial tour guide, I pointed out historic buildings that were covered with clouds -- Buckingham Palace, the clocktower of Big Ben, the vaulted rooftops of Parliament, and so forth.

Then Annie pointed straight down at something far more obvious -- the ice cream truck at the entrance to the London Eye. My three other children quickly followed suit. They saw no point in trying to make out the distant, shady little shapes behind the clouds. They wanted ice cream. They couldn't have cared less about the famous London skyline.

Then it hit me: Like most investors, I had been so preoccupied with interpreting murky economic indicators and the jittery stock market indexes that I had lost sight of the most obvious things – the stocks I owned. Instead of listening to hand-wringing pundits complain about European banks, I should have been asking questions like, "How many iPhones is Apple selling in China?" Buying companies that were not being battered by Europe's woes – and had a brighter future elsewhere -- would have been a far more productive use of my time.

Four months later, I was forced to focus on the smaller picture just as my children had taught me on the London Eye. On March 11, 2011, the Fukushima Daiichi Nuclear Power Plant suffered major damage from a magnitude 9.0 earthquake and tsunami in the northern Tohoku region of Japan. That's when I received an email from a broker that said, "Do not buy anything right now. ... This reactor is out of control, we are hearing from a very reliable source." Sure enough, on April 20th, 2011, Japanese authorities evacuated everyone within 20 kilometers from the power plant. In the ensuing panic, the S&P 500 index fell 3.5 percent. Louis Vuitton shares fell even farther, by 12 percent, on fears that high-end Japanese consumers would be afraid to venture out to the upmarket stores that sold the company's luxury goods.

The broker was telling us to hit the button and sell everything. I ignored his advice. Instead, I learned that you always need to work out how much of a company's revenue comes from the country affected by a natural disaster before you decide not to buy it. I knew Louis Vuitton derived only 9 percent of its sales from Japan -- though it considered that country to be an important market -- and I decided that the company would not be hurt in the long term. So I hit the button and bought the stock. "The unexpected" happens more often than you think, which allows you to make money through long-term trends and use selloffs as an opportunity to find an entry point into a hot stock that had previously been too expensive to buy. By April 2011, Louis Vuitton was one of my fund's biggest positions, having posted very strong first quarter sales globally.

In October 2011, I got to thinking about the English Channel around Jersey, where friends who sailed their boats complained that there were several treacherous rocks that could easily sink them. With thorough planning, they said, the rocks were perfectly avoidable. In the stock market, though, investors had started crashing into a big, sharp, dangerous rock called Greece. In response, many other investors had pulled their boats out of the water. But my thorough planning meant that I could enjoy navigating the waters while avoiding such risks.

Greece made me think of friends who ask me to lend them money even though they're still throwing parties and taking vacations every year. My opinion of them fell even lower than it had been previously. Like Greece, they insisted on spending borrowed money, and they were unwilling to change. The implied threat was that if the rest of Europe didn't bail Greece out, it would never be able to repay what it had already borrowed, which would drag the rest of Europe down under the rocks.

In July 2011, I wrote in my monthly newsletter for investors in my fund: "Simple strategy: We want to invest in only those industries supported by a strong, durable macro-economic theme: growth must be abundant. We want to buy businesses that sustain their profit margins (whether derived from branding, market position, pricing power). When growth comes easily to a company, and pricing power is evident, future profits of the business are so easy to imagine that financial markets eventually treat them as certainty."

Like clockwork, that month Apple announced that its four stores in mainland China were officially the most heavily trafficked Apple Stores in the world.

Unfortunately, opportunities to make a killing like that on purely European stocks became increasingly scarce over the years. In fact, so much went so badly wrong. While the U.S. had pulled itself out of its financial crisis in 2010, governments across the continent spent several years bailing themselves out of debt. The Eurozone debt crisis never seemed to end, and the stock market was intent on punishing everyone for it. In 2011, the MSCI Europe Index fell 10.5 percent, and it slipped again for three years from 2014 to 2016.

Europe had become almost a dirty word in the stock market even before the UK voted to secede from the EU in June 2016. Brexit, as the ordeal was known, was quite draining. My colleagues, clients and everyone else constantly talked about it. It sapped the energy out of the hedge fund business. Every single time it came up, the business became less enjoyable.

It became abundantly clear that Europe was no place for a hedge fund manager. The growth opportunities are all in U.S.-based companies that are disrupting global industries with new technology. They're making their money around the world --

only partly in Europe, where my kids use some of their products every day. Nevertheless, they're not European companies, and I was managing a European fund with a mandate to invest primarily in European stocks.

I could not see a way forward for hedge funds – not just in Europe, but worldwide -- and it was no more encouraging than the future I saw for the laundromat business in Liverpool with the simple mind of a 14-year-old. Hedge funds started to look a lot like a laundromat to me. It was clear that the days when you could set up a hedge fund from scratch were over. Today, you could say the business is quite extinct.

The truth is that the hedge fund industry has not kept up with the performance of the S&P 500. Most funds charge their clients 2 percent of assets under management – that is, just to park their money somewhere. In addition, they collect 20 percent of performance – that is, if there is any performance to speak of.

Thanks to the internet, you can do it all yourself. You can get almost all the information you need to make a decision to invest in any company or industry from Google – not Google Finance, just the search engine. You can buy Exchange Traded Funds (ETFs) that invest in almost any theme you can think of, from environmental social and governance (ESG) issues to hot commodities like nickel and copper. You can even bet against entire industries by shorting individual stocks through an online broker like Charles Schwab, which will even help you borrow the shares in a margin account.

Almost everyone has lost faith in hedge funds. Ever since Bernie Madoff, a former chairman of NASDAQ, was sentenced to 150 years in prison in 2009, for reporting fake returns of 10 to 12 percent year after year. Investors who had been told their principal had grown found out that they hadn't made a profit at all – and that they weren't going to get any money back, either. The vast majority of hedge funds were not obliged to report their holdings to regulatory authorities, so investors in most hedge funds couldn't see what was inside the kitchen.

That lack of trust led to a tsunami of new regulation, which has multiplied the costs of running a hedge fund. Mountains of red tape and back-office reporting now consume hours of a portfolio manager's time every day. This has made the whole business much less lucrative and a lot less exciting.

Without a doubt, the 10 percent minority of hedge fund managers who do outperform really are doing the job the way it's supposed to be done. They are going to be worth their weight in gold for the foreseeable future. However, those hedge funds tend to be closed to new investors. If you're not a pension fund, odds are you'll never get in -- even if you can afford the $100,000 or $1 million initial deposit required of high net worth investors.

I was proud to have been in a great industry when the barriers to entry for setting up a hedge fund were very low. This enabled talented managers with little capital to set up hedge funds and demonstrate their ability. Today, the cost of setting up a hedge fund will unfortunately deter young, talented risk-takers from setting up their own hedge fund business. They were once the industry's life blood. Today, I'm even prouder to be investing for my own family – without the responsibility of managing a hedge fund business day after day.

CHAPTER TWENTY-FOUR: STAYING AHEAD OF THE CURVE

After my father passed away in 2018, my mother turned his dwindling laundromat business over to me. The first thing I did was shut down the three remaining branches.

As I mentioned at the beginning of the book, I stepped down as the portfolio manager of my hedge fund, liquidated the fund, and returned all the cash to investors in late February 2020. Those who had stayed with the fund since its inception in 2005 enjoyed a annualized return of more than 8 percent. Over that period of time, the Euro Stoxx 50 index was more or less unchanged. However, those who left early – or came late to the party – might not have fared so well.

From my experience of managing a fund, investors always seemed to invest at the wrong time. These investors remind me of the time when I took my second eldest child, Maisie, fishing on the north coast of Wales. As soon as she had cast her fishing rod, she asked, "How long will it take to catch a fish?" I explained that it takes time and patience. About ten minutes later, she wanted to reel in her line and buy an almond Magnum from the ice cream truck on the beach.

She reminded me of some of my investors who would get terribly impatient if they didn't see an almost immediate return on their investment. This leads to costly and irrational decisions even though the fundamental picture has not changed. All I could do is explain that it can take months for a stock to rise or fall – while they closed their accounts and went off looking for a fund manager who could promise them instant returns.

Just like my investors, Maisie got impatient when fishing. She would rather have been doing other things – like getting her favorite ice cream from the ice-cream van. This would have given her immediate satisfaction rather than the satisfaction that you have to wait for -- like catching a fish. Like some of my investors, she didn't understand that it was a waiting game.

Now that my three decades of managing hedge funds in Europe's stock markets and making markets in European stocks are safely behind me, and I am no longer managing outside capital, I have the freedom to invest in anything I want for my family office.

I've already talked about the companies I invest in because they are disrupting industries with the technology they have developed, like Tesla, Facebook, Amazon and Netflix. Looking forward, the challenge will be to identify the disruptors of the technology that gave these companies an advantage in the stock market. What, for example, will replace the digital Times Square that Facebook built in Cyberspace, the streaming movies on Netflix and Disney+, or the touchless purchasing power of Amazon Go?

Within the living memory of my children, the one factor that will probably remain a constant is that new players will always displace old players with new technology. The only question will be from where the next disruption will arise. As technologically advanced as our daily lives are becoming, you will never have to be a rocket scientist to figure out how to stay ahead of the curve.

What can help you stay ahead of the curve is viewing countries as stocks. It could be argued that if my mandate hadn't been that of a European equity manager, my performance could have been better. Simply choosing the right countries to invest in can put you massively ahead of the game. This is something Warren Buffett is a big advocate of; he has used the U.S. economy as a major tailwind.

Let's start with the U.S., where the economy is effectively the owner of many great internet businesses that emerged from the financial crisis of 2008 in extremely good health. Since then, the U.S. economy has grown by 40 percent. The U.S. enjoyed record low unemployment rates prior to COVID-19, and it's fair to say that America is still a superpower when it comes to technology.

The U.S. will remain a powerhouse while Japan continues to struggle. America is leading the global race because its corporations never lost their knack for creating brands that target the global market and execute perfectly. Consumers anywhere can connect with American brands like Starbucks, which is enjoying its most furious growth in China. Young people seem to forget that coffee shops are still a relatively new phenomenon. Starbucks appeals to every culture around the world, along with other American brands such as McDonald's and Coca-Cola.

Just as importantly, America is leading the world in the development of new technology. Some of the world's most carefully calculated investments are pouring into Silicon Valley to develop products for Apple, Google, Facebook, and Visa. America's rate of innovation is faster than any other country.

One thing that came out of COVID-19 was that American workers want to work so badly that they protested for the right to go back to work. These were people who did not want to stay home and collect unemployment insurance. Culturally, this shows me that Americans are driven. They are hard working.

Now let's look at Europe, where the regulatory framework has been more stringent than that of the U.S. The region has produced very few tech companies. SAP, Europe's biggest company, is capitalized at only $110 billion, which is only one-tenth the size of Microsoft.

As I'm sure you've noticed, statues in public squares tend to depict individuals. I can't think of a statue that depicts an entire committee. Unfortunately, the European Union is one big committee, and its 27 members have not been communicating with each other since the UK seceded. When you buy a stock in Europe, with the exception of luxury brands, you are effectively buying into a dysfunctional committee.

Even though the U.S. population of 328 million is slightly less than half of Europe's population of 741.4 million, Europe's GDP is actually 30 percent less than that of the U.S. As of July

2020, Europe's economy is even smaller than it was during the financial crisis of 2008.

Europe isn't done with economic debacles. There are still quite a few issues in the pipeline that will rival Brexit in terms of their potential to destabilize the EU. In countries like Italy, the national debt is still 30 percent larger than the economy – and they have no real plan to reduce it. This will result in unforeseen problems later. As long as Europe is led by competing leaders, it will be difficult for the Continent to unite.

Going forward, Europe will need to be run under a single set of rules. A good start would be to write one taxation rulebook that all 27 member states of the EU can live by. Just look at the differences in the current corporate tax rates from country to country, which range from 12.5 percent in Ireland to 28 percent in France. They need to unite. If they don't, their lunch will be eaten by the Americans or the Chinese, who are continuing to grow and innovate.

A stronger union would prepare Europe to face its next crisis, which is likely to be triggered by immigration from hotspots in the Middle East. Two EU member states, Bulgaria and Greece, share borders with Turkey. Turkey's other neighbors are Syria, Iraq, Iran, and Afghanistan, all of which have been torn by wars that have flooded Europe with refugees. One of those countries, Afghanistan, is home to the region's largest refugee population, hosting more than 4 million men, women and children in more than twenty refugee camps.

That's the leverage that Turkey has over Europe. If the EU refuses to meet Turkey's demands for billions of euros in "aid" every year, Turkey threatens to release Afghanistan's 4 million refugees across the continent.

It's not only the refugees in Afghanistan that Europe has to worry about. Immigration from the Middle East will become more of a burden on Europe as oil prices continue to fall and the economies of Iran and Iraq, both of which export oil, continue to suffer. COVID-19 gouged oil prices when airlines were grounded, and factories came to a standstill worldwide. Now that the oil money has stopped flowing through these economies, immigration can only increase. It's only a matter of time before people are forced to flee Iran and Iraq, where millions of them can no longer afford food, clothing or shelter.

Turkey could throw a curve ball across the border of the EU at any moment. The Turkish Lira has fallen over 50 percent against the dollar since 2016, placing a great strain on Turkey's economy. To make matters worse, President Recep Tayyip Erdogan is starting to lose the support of his own people. As a result, Turkey could plunge into civil war at any time. That would leave no country in the Middle East with any economic prospects, consequently putting pressure on Europe.

Now let's look more closely at Japan, which rose from the radioactive ashes of the Second World War by building the foundation of its economy on the manufacturing of cars, cameras, and consumer electronics. Japan also pioneered miniaturization, starting with the Sony Walkman in the Seventies. By the Eighties, most office desks in London had a Casio calculator and a Toshiba landline. It became *de rigueur* to wear a Casio digital watch, drive a Toyota to work, and watch the TV news on a Sony Trinitron.

Yet when my family and I visited Japan in 2015, it was clear that the Land of the Rising Sun had not embraced – much less invested in -- current Western technology. Today, Japan is producing no new technology or brands, and in some ways the country is falling behind South Korea. Japan got stuck in a cycle of just trying to make things cheaper without innovating or create new ways of doing things. Companies became obsessed with just-in-time mass production and making things cheaper, which is ultimately a zero-sum game.

Now the top smartphone companies -- Apple, Samsung and Huawei – are all from the U.S., Korea or China. The mobile phone has completely displaced the consumer electronics industry of Japan. No one is listening to music on a Sony Walkman anymore. Instead, people are far more likely to be is listening to Spotify on an iPhone with Apple Air Pods. Samsung of Korea uses Google's Android operating system. Even simple things like a calculator or flashlight have been replaced by smartphones. The smartphone has obliterated many Japanese jobs, and American businesses are behind it.

The Japanese auto industry has been no more encouraging. It's been more than two decades since Toyota rolled out the Prius, the world's first hybrid gasoline-electric car. Since then, Honda, Mazda, Nissan, Toyota, and Suzuki have started to feel like worn-out brands.

If you wouldn't buy a Japanese car, you shouldn't buy shares in the company that manufactures it. Shares of Nissan have fallen over 60 percent, which could make the stock look cheap, but think again: Would you rather drive a Nissan or a Tesla? It would not surprise me if the share prices of Japanese carmakers performed no better than other companies related to the petroleum industry in the years to come.

However, I am not completely writing off Japan. We should stay alert for any new technology that comes out of that country. In particular, keep an eye on gaming, where companies like Nintendo are thriving.

China is going to be far more interesting for investors than Japan. China's gross domestic product has increased from $3 trillion in 2000 to $13 trillion today. This ranks China among the top three superpowers in economic terms.

The key to China's success is clear leadership. China is perceived as being run by seven men. Not unlike a corporate board of directors, the Politburo Standing Committee is effective because it engenders rapid decision making. China's population of 1.39 billion does not appear to slow them down. In sharp contrast, the EU has 27 members – far too many to come to a quick decision.

Despite the international outrage that greeted the suppression of whistleblowers who tried to warn Chinese authorities in the early days of the pandemic, the government responded quickly when the story finally got out. It took only ten days to build the 1,000-bed Huoshenshan Hospital for COVID-19 patients. The Chinese have demonstrated fantastic organizational skills.

Now let's say Europe and the three countries I've discussed above were stocks. If I were to rank them in a portfolio as I ask the interns at my office to do, I would rank the U.S. as No. 1, followed by China in second place. Then I would have to flip a coin for third and fourth place -- between Europe and Japan. If I were to invest in any of their currencies over the long term, I would hold on the U.S. dollar and the Chinese Renminbi. To stay ahead of the curve, I would just focus on the U.S. stock market.

CHAPTER TWENTY-FIVE: CATCHING THE NEXT WAVE

In the end, what watersports in Jersey have taught me is that investing is a close cousin to surfing. If you catch the right wave by investing in the right stock, then it's an exhilarating experience. Once you have tasted the exhilaration of an epic wave, you can't wait to ride the next one. The skill of a great surfer is knowing how to pick the right wave. If you pick the wrong one, the best one may be right behind you – but by then it's too late to catch it. Whichever wave you wind up riding, you'll have to start planning a smooth exit before you wipe out.

In the stock market, there are times when you just have to accept that you may have caught three big waves, but the conditions aren't right to catch a fourth one. That can be hard to accept when the adrenaline is flowing. I caught the wrong wave when I invested in European banks. I had fun riding that wave from 2012 to 2015 amid expectations that we were at the bottom of the interest rate cycle. With interest rates near zero, how much lower could they really go? As it turned out, the European Central Bank (ECB) decided to keep its main refinancing rate at 0.0 percent and carried on printing endless amounts of euros, leaving everyone under the impression that rates would stay in deep freeze for another generation. This led to a dramatic downgrading of European banks in 2016.

What this taught me is that if you are playing a cyclical part of the market that is particularly sensitive to the economy, such as banks and mining companies, if you don't get the timing right, the wave just crashes over your head when prices fall. Value investors who have been drawn into the oil and gas industry, banks, and mining companies have all been punished recently.

Thanks to the convergence of the internet with the real economy, the economic cycle is producing significant deflationary pressure. Prices are falling because anyone can shop online, and the cheapest price always wins. Largely because of the internet ultra-loose monetary policy is just not producing the much-needed inflation, which is making it extremely difficult for anyone to invest their hard-earned money in anything. While the internet has been a great wave to surf, its ripple effects have destroyed many industries in its wake.

In short, you can make money in a downturn if you see it as an opportunity -- and you don't procrastinate too long. So, in March this year, I retired at 47 and formed my own family office. I work from home, which I am extremely fortunate to do as it allows me to interact with my friends and family on a daily basis.

It wasn't just that I saw no need to work myself into the grave in an extinct business as my father did. As I explained earlier, I wanted to free myself up to invest in the U.S. stock market. That's where the growth is -- even in the wake of the worst pandemic since the Spanish flu of 1917 and the most rapid and severe stock market collapse since 1987. I am investing in the future that my children are building for themselves through the way they interact with businesses that are replacing those I grew up with, from banks to movie theaters to supermarkets.

From my children's perspective, there has been little positive to say about investing. They haven't seen much of an opportunity. They've heard about greedy bankers, the collapse of Europe's stock market, rising unemployment, and even the secession of the country of their birth from Continental Europe. They've seen a lot of disenfranchised people.

But they don't have to be among the disenfranchised – and neither do you. Next time you shout at your children for playing computer games, think again and ask them what game it is and which company makes it. If one of your friends shows you a new fitness app, find out which company is behind it and what makes it unique. Just be aware of the companies you and your friends and family are interacting with on a daily basis -- and whether you can buy shares in them. If you choose not to invest, you might just send your resume to them instead. Above all, do your best not to get stuck in a business that could become a laundromat.

Life is too short. Don't over complicate your life. It can be simpler than you think.

Jacket Blurb:

What do Greta Thunberg, Elon Musk and Warren Buffett have in common? As far apart as they may seem, these global icons represent key themes in Stephen Roberts' time-tested approach to picking stocks with such common sense that teenagers are now using it to build their future after COVID-19.

ABOUT THE AUTHOR

Stephen Roberts

Stephen was a former partner and portfolio manager for Horseman Capital. Horseman Capital was renowned in the hedge fund industry for its high conviction thematic approach to investing. Stephen now runs his own family office.

Contact:
Email: srobertsjersey@gmail.com
Twitter: @itssimplerthan1
Instagram: @itssimplerthanyouthink

ABOUT THE AUTHOR

Annie Roberts

Annie Roberts is 19 years old and is reading Business Management at Edinburgh University. Growing up around her father she felt it was important to encourage others not to be overwhelmed by the stock market and instead to look at it simply.

Contact:
Email: annieroberts083@yahoo.com
Twitter: @itssimplerthan1
Instagram: @itssimplerthanyouthink

Printed in Poland
by Amazon Fulfillment
Poland Sp. z o.o., Wrocław